Psychology for Church Leaders Series

MAN IN MOTION

The Psychology of Human Motivation

Gary R. Collins

CREATION HOUSE
CAROL STREAM, ILLINOIS

FIRST EDITION

Library of Congress Catalog Card Number: 72-94832

Acknowledgments

The author gratefully acknowledges the cooperation of the following publishers who have given written permission to quote from the sources listed below:

Concordia Publishing House — For excerpts from Paul Meehl, et. al., *What, Then, is Man?* Copyright 1958.

William B. Eerdmans Publishers—For excerpts from G. C. Berkouwer, *Man: The Image of God*, Copyright 1962.

Harper & Row Publishers — For excerpts from Simon Doniger, *The Nature of Man in Theological and Psychological Perspective*, Copyright 1962.

His magazine— For excerpts from Vernon Grounds. "Psychiatry and Christianity: Conversion," November, 1963. Copyright Inter-Varsity Christian Fellowship.

Zondervan Publishing House—For excerpts from Stuart Barton Babbage, *The Vacuum of Unbelief*, Copyright 1969.

CONTENTS

Preface

For a lot of people, life today is boring, meaningless, and filled with frustration. Newspapers carry stories about drug use and pollution, there appears to be a breakdown in law and order, prices and taxes seem to be spiraling upward, and the individual often feels that he is powerless to bring about any kind of change. Some people try to find hope in horoscopes, occultism, or the mystical eastern religions; others become excessively busy in order to hide from the futility of their lives and society; some escape with drugs or alcohol; and if we can believe the existential philosophers, an increasing number are giving up in despair and concluding that nothing in the world makes sense anymore.

This prevailing attitude of hopelessness and frustration presents the church with one of its greatest challenges: to get people interested, enthusiastic, and involved in spiritual issues. In an attempt to encourage and motivate individuals many congregations are experimenting with creative new forms of church renewal, but all of these efforts involve people and this gets us into the area of psychology.

As a modern science, psychology is a vast and complex field which has as its subject matter the whole spectrum of human and animal behavior. While much of the psychologist's work—including most animal research—has no bearing on the ministry of the church, there is a lot of psychology which can be and often is very helpful.

In *Man in Transition, Fractured Personalities,* and *Effective Counseling*—the first three volumes in the "Psychology for Church Leaders" series—we have attempted to show how the church can benefit from a better understanding of normal human development, abnormal behavior, and the techniques of counseling. These three topics have special relevance for the church leader, and it is probably for this reason that these are the topics which most often

9

appear in books and articles about pastoral counseling. But these are not the only pertinent psychological issues. To have ended the present series after the third volume would have been to leave out a large and significant segment of psychology—a segment which the field of pastoral psychology tends to neglect—how people differ from one another, how people see the world, how they experience and show emotions, how they can be motivated, and how they get along or why they don't get along with one another. These all are important topics which have been carefully studied in psychological experiments, with results that can be of practical value to the church leader.

When a college student enrolls in a beginning psychology course he learns about these experiments and he encounters all of the issues that we have mentioned above. Sometimes, however, the psychology courses are not very stimulating or exciting, but to a large extent this is because of the very nature of science itself. By definition, scientific experiments must be precise and carefully controlled. When these experiments are completed and described in professional journals, the reports are often very detailed and in highly technical language. To the non-psychologist (and to many psychologists as well) these articles are often dull and meaningless.

Hidden in the technical jargon of numerous psychological journals, however, is a wealth of very practical information which need not be boring or irrelevant at all. This information can stimulate and assist the church leader in his or her efforts to understand, help and motivate modern man. It is this information—the how, what, why, when, and where of general psychology—which we will discuss in the pages which follow.

1

How People Change:
The Psychology of Teaching and Learning

If we were to select one word that could summarize the earthly ministry of Jesus, "teaching" would be a good choice. Jesus taught His followers about Himself, about the Father and the Holy Spirit, about the Scriptures, about the future, and about God's great plan of redemption. Often He was given the name "teacher" (or "rabbi," which means the same thing), and at the end of His life when He was giving last instructions to the believers, Jesus told them to go forth and teach (Mt. 28:20).

Throughout history Christians have attempted to follow this directive. Sunday schools, vacation Bible schools, youth clubs, Christian colleges, Bible institutes, and theological seminaries have been established to instruct the young in the truths of Scripture. Hundreds of thousands of sermons have presented the message of Christ and in countless homes Christian parents have taught their children about Jesus.

In order to learn, people do not always need to have a teacher. Scientists learn by doing experiments, athletes learn by continual practice, and at times all of us learn from experience or trial and error. But a teacher can speed up the learning and make it more efficient. How he can best do this, and how his students can learn more effectively have concerned philosophers and other thinking men for centuries. More recently psychologists and educators have done literally thousands of experiments on human learning, and the results of these investigations are of great importance to the Christian parent or teacher.

How Learning Occurs

Earlier in the twentieth century, psychologists held a number of theories about how learning occurs. When these theories were subjected to rigid experimental study, many of them collapsed, but research has now shown that learning usually occurs in two basic ways. [1]

CLASSICAL CONDITIONING

Perhaps the best known experiment in the history of psychology was done by a man who wasn't a psychologist. Ivan Pavlov was a Russian physiologist who had won a Nobel prize for his studies of digestion. Pavlov worked with dogs and in order to study the flow of saliva into the mouth. He had surgically inserted a little tube into the animals' cheeks. It was well known that the dogs would produce saliva when they tasted food, but Pavlov discovered something else— the animals began to salivate as soon as they came into the laboratory. Apparently the dogs had learned that coming into the laboratory would be followed by food so they salivated in anticipation long before the food appeared. In his famous experiments Pavlov studied this systematically. He rang a little bell (perhaps we could call it a dinner bell) and then gave food to the dog. The sound of the bell, which previously had brought forth no saliva, became associated or linked with food and before long, the bell itself caused the animals to salivate in anticipation.

Impressed with Pavlov's findings some early experimenters decided to see if the same type of learning could occur in humans. We know, of course, that our mouths water when we think of food or look at a menu and one researcher even tried to collect saliva from the mouths of people (without cutting holes in their cheeks, I am happy to report). [2] Later other ways were devised to study this kind of learning in humans. In one such study an eleven-month-old boy named Albert was shown a white rat. Initially Albert showed no fear of the animal and eagerly reached out to touch and pet it. Then the experimenters sounded a loud noise and Albert shrank back. By presenting the rat and then the noise several times, Albert soon reacted with fear whenever he saw the rat. He had learned to associate the rat with a fear-arousing noise.[3]

Apparently a lot of learning occurs in this way. Some kind of a stimulation (like a bell or little animal) that originally didn't influence us much, gets linked with a stimulus that does affect our behavior (like food or a fearful noise). Before long the neutral stimulus becomes influential, just like the bell and animal eventually came to affect behavior. This is known as classical conditioning.

Through classical conditioning, we learn many of our fears and attitudes. Consider, for example, how people develop a fear of snakes. Little children are rarely afraid of snakes, but by the time they reach adulthood most people *are* afraid.[4] To understand how this fear is developed by conditioning it is important to remember that whenever an adult reacts with horror, fear, or some other emotion, a child will pick this up and react in a similar manner. Originally the snake does not frighten the child, but when he sees the adult's fear, the child learns to link "snakes" with "something to be afraid of." The fear of snakes is learned in childhood and persists into adulthood. A fear of lightning or flying, a dislike of some minority group, or a preference for certain food can all be learned in much the same way.

Happily, we can also condition people to *not* fear. In the experiment with little Albert, the researchers removed the fear by presenting the rat and then giving the child pleasant-tasting food instead of a noise. Before long the rat became associated with pleasant things again and the fear disappeared.

13

What does all of this have to do with Christian education? In all likelihood, we learn many attitudes about the Scriptures, God, and moral standards by seeing how parents and teachers react. "God" is just a meaningless word to a little child, but he learns to respect and revere God if this attitude is shown by the parents. The child finds meaning in his world by seeing how other people react to events and stimulations.

Some psychologists question whether much human learning can be explained in terms of classical conditioning, and in a technical discussion it could be argued that the above examples are not conditioning at all. More relevant for our purposes as Christian educators, therefore, is the second type of learning.

INSTRUMENTAL LEARNING

In a recent survey, 1000 members of the American Psychological Association were asked to name the most important figure in contemporary psychology. An overwhelming majority gave the name of B. F. Skinner, and next to Freud, Skinner was selected as the individual who has had the greatest influence on psychology in the 20th century. [5]

Skinner's reputation among his colleagues arose from his work with pigeons. In his laboratory at Harvard, Skinner discovered that if a pellet of food was given periodically, a pigeon could be trained to do all sorts of things—like pecking a disk, distinguishing between different colors or shapes, turning circles, or even selecting defective pills from a conveyor belt. The food which rewarded the animal for his behavior is known as *reinforcement*. Technically defined, a reinforcement is any object or event which causes an animal to repeat the action for which he was reinforced—but it is probably easier to think of "reinforcement" as being roughly equivalent to "reward." Instrumental learning is that kind of learning in which an individual makes a response which is followed by reinforcement.

On a human level, much of our behavior is molded by

14

reinforcement. When a child takes his first step, says a word or two, gets an *A* on a test in school, or plays "Jesus Loves Me" on the piano, the parents usually respond with praise and acclaim. This praise reinforces the child and causes him to repeat the desirable behavior. If a preacher tries a new way to prepare his sermon and discovers that people are responsive, he is likely to repeat his new technique. If the people are critical or not responsive, the pastor drops the new behavior because it has not been reinforced. Sometimes we even reinforce ourselves. "If I can read fifty pages before lunch," the student thinks, "I'll go to the game this afternoon."

On the basis of Skinner's work and that of his students, a number of learning principles have been discovered. At first these were known to apply only to pigeons, but psychological research has now shown that the same principles which account for animal learning also apply to a great deal of human learning. We will look at a few of these principles in more detail because they have a direct bearing on Christian education. [6]

As long as a subject is given reinforcement, he will continue indefinitely with the behavior for which he is reinforced. Give food to a pigeon for pecking a little spot on the wall in his cage, and he'll continue to peck. Give a dog a biscuit for sitting on his hind legs and he'll continue to do this "trick" whenever you want—or at least until he is tired of canine crackers.

Although some readers may feel uncomfortable with the idea, we know that this same principle applies to people. Give a child some candy or words of praise for some accomplishment and he will repeat the behavior. If he throws a tantrum demanding to stay up past his bedtime, let him get away with it and you have reinforced his tantrum behavior, making it likely that he will try this tactic again. Skinner has concluded that teaching today is often ineffective because busy teachers do not and cannot reinforce the child whenever he does something correctly. To improve teaching, Skinner suggests,[7] we must find a way to reinforce the learner whenever he makes a desirable response.

This principle or reinforcement can apply to all types of human learning. Think, for example, of discussion groups. Some group leaders seem to have great skill at getting a discussion going, while other leaders fail miserably. Whether he realizes it or not, the effective group leader makes great use of reinforcement. If a group member makes a statement, the good leader expresses appreciation for the comment—by words or gestures such as a smile and head nod—and the speaker, having been reinforced, is inclined to participate again. Before long, the group members are reinforcing each other. They may not agree with each other's comments, but they do encourage (i.e., reinforce) each other for contributing. If a person talks too much, however, the reinforcement from others is likely to stop. By giving desirable reinforcements whenever a person does something that is acceptable, and by not giving reinforcement when the person shows unacceptable behavior, psychologists have been able to help mental patients to get better; teach disturbed children how to talk and relate to others; eliminate thumbsucking, stealing, crying, tantrums, stuttering, excessive vomiting, and social withdrawal in children; control overeating; eliminate fears; train retarded people; and get rid of undesirable sex behavior.[8] To be quite frank, the effective use of reinforcement is a very successful way to change and even control the behavior of others.[9]

Reinforcement speeds up learning. It is possible to learn without reinforcement (psychologists call this "latent learning") but this is often a slow and inefficient process. By reinforcing desirable behavior, learning is speeded up considerably.

The type of reinforcement is important. Pigeons learn very quickly if they are reinforced with grains or water, but they don't learn very well if given raisins or something that they don't like. The same is true with people. Promise a college student an *A* for completing some assignment and he will work harder than if you promise him a quarter or an ice cream cone. For the second-grade student, however, the reverse may be true, and this illustrates the important point that what is reinforcing to one person may not be reinforcing to another.

The story is told of an elementary school in which the students were rowdy and poorly behaved. In an attempt to restore law and order the principal decided to award a banner to the class that was "best behaved during the month." For the younger students, those in grades one, two, and three, the change was remarkable. They wanted to win the banner and so they became very well-behaved. The older students, in contrast, couldn't think of anything more humiliating than to win a good-behavior banner and these children, if anything, were more poorly behaved than they had been before.

As children grow older there is a change in what they find reinforcing. This has practical implications for parents and for Sunday school teachers. Contests and the promise of bookmarks or other prizes work well with some groups, but not with others. Here again we see the role of individual differences. What reinforces one may have no reinforcing influence at all with somebody else.

In any teaching situation, we should seek to find what is most reinforcing to the individual or age group with whom we are working. Banners, bookmarks, grades, money, and food have already been mentioned but we must also recognize that the subject matter itself can be reinforcing. Children play for long periods with water, sand, scissors, or puzzles, not because they will receive some outside reward for doing this but because it is reinforcing just to manipulate these objects in the environment. Students sometimes begin to study with the expectation that they will get praise or tangible rewards for their efforts, but later they find that studying is reinforcing in itself. Some people work long hours, not because they need money or security, but primarily because they enjoy their work.

The time of reinforcement is important. If food is given immediately after a pigeon pecks a disk, he will keep on pecking at a steady rate. If he has a long wait between the peck and the coming of the food, he soon gives up and stops pecking.

To some extent this principle also applies to people. The student who writes a paper or test for his professor, and then has to wait two months before it is graded, loses much of the value of the assignment. The preacher who stresses the Christian's rewards in heaven is putting a big gap between present behavior and future reinforcement. Perhaps this is why Jesus also stressed the value of an abundant Christian life *now*, in the present (Jn. 10:10).

Unlike animals, however, people are able to endure a longer gap between behavior and reinforcement. This is because we have language. There is a very long waiting period between the student's studying in school and the higher status and income that is supposed to come because he got an education. But he keeps studying, partly because of the reinforcement that he experiences now—like grades or a feeling of accomplishment—and partly because he is able to understand that other rewards will come his way in the future.

Once behavior has been learned, it is not necessary to give reinforcement after every response. As long as reinforcement comes periodically, the animal will keep responding for a long period of time. Skinner once had a pigeon who made 20,000 pecks at a disk even though the animal only received a total of thirty-six reinforcements.

Anyone who has walked along the streets in downtown Las Vegas will see this principle at work with people. As long as somebody wins periodically, the gambler keeps putting money into the machine or onto the betting table in hopes that he will be next. In the home or school the same principle applies. If parents give in to a temper tantrum occasionally, the child will persist in this behavior even though he doesn't *always* get what he wants. The student will keep studying and the housewife or her husband will keep working, even though reinforcements don't always follow their efforts. To some extent the same is true of our Christian experience. Many believers continue to spend time in regular prayer and Bible study, recognizing that sometimes this gives us a real lift but that other times it doesn't seem to influence us much.

When reinforcement stops completely, so does behavior. The pigeon won't peck forever if he doesn't receive food and neither will a person respond in the complete absence of reinforcement. Returning again to the problem of temper tantrums, these will disappear if the child discovers that he never gets what he wants by throwing a tantrum. If a Sunday school class is always dull or the church is seen as irrelevant (that is, nonreinforcing), the student will drop out, concluding that it makes no sense to come to church if this doesn't meet one's needs. This may account for the recent revival of the "underground church." Thousands of young people find Christianity more exciting and challenging—that means more reinforcing—in small and lively groups than in the dead atmosphere of a staid church.

Of course some people go to church even when they claim to "get nothing from it." It may be, however, that these people really are getting some reinforcement. To avoid church might arouse guilt feelings and it feels better (more reinforcing) to attend habitually than to stay at home on Sunday. 10

WHAT ABOUT PUNISHMENT?

To this point we have stressed the importance of reinforcing desirable behavior and withholding reinforcement when the behavior is undesirable. But what about punishment?

Doesn't a spanking or severe tongue-lashing influence behavior? Doesn't keeping a child after school or giving a *D* to a lazy student have some influence on behavior?

King Solomon certainly favored punishment (Pr. 13:24; 22:15; 23:13; 29:15) but for a long time psychologists did not. Skinner once wrote a best-selling novel [11] in which he indicated that after untold human suffering, we now are discovering that punishment does not reduce undesirable behavior at all. Other writers have suggested that punishment is cruel and unnecessary, a poor controller of behavior, and the cause at times of neuroses. [12]

It is now clear that in most situations punishment *does* stop behavior, but only temporarily. Punish an animal, child, or criminal and almost invariably he stops the undesirable behavior for a while but then repeats it later when he is left on his own. There is a way to make the effects of punishment more permanent, however. If we punish undesirable behavior and then, while the behavior is suppressed, show the person how to reach his goals by a more desirable route, punishment is effective. Stated another way, we can say that efficient learning comes if we punish the behavior which we don't like and then immediately follow this up by reinforcing behavior which we do like. If a child steals from the cookie jar he gets spanked, but he learns that if he then asks politely he gets what he wanted. Here we punish the wrong response and reinforce that which is right.

Few topics in the field of learning, indeed in the whole of psychology, are more complicated than the issue of punishment, but research is continuing and hopefully in the future we will know more about this than we do now. [13]

TRANSFER OR "CARRY-OVER"

As part of their training for space travel, astronauts spend long hours in simulators. These are devices which in many respects resemble a real space capsule except that they remain on the ground. It is assumed that what the spacemen can learn in a phony vehicle will carry over or, to use the psychological term, "transfer" to the real situation. Closer to our own experience we assume that if a person learns to drive a Dodge, his driving skills will go with him when he gets behind the wheel of a Ford. As a teacher, I hope that the things my students learn in class will carry over and be of practical value outside of the classroom. Indeed, all of education—including that which takes place in the home, church, or seminary—is based on the assumption that transfer does and will occur.

Psychologists have identified two kinds of transfer. *Positive transfer* is the kind we have been discussing. Here what we learn in one area carries over to help us in the learning or performance of some other task. *Negative transfer* is just the opposite. What we learn in one situation hinders or interferes with our learning in another situation. The seminary student who studies Hebrew and Greek during the same semester, and gets the two mixed up, is experiencing negative transfer. What is being learned in one class is interfering with what the student is learning in another. Ideally, effective education should be characterized by a lot of positive carry-over (or transfer) and a minimum of negative transfer.

How do we make sure that positive transfer will occur? The following suggestions are based on research into this problem. [14]

Try to make the teaching situation and the later situation as similar as possible. Theological students who are studying homiletics often are required to prepare and deliver a sermon in front of a "congregation" of classmates. To the extent that the classroom situation is similar to the later parish setting, transfer will occur. A summer of practical experience as a ministerial assistant lets future pastors learn in a situation which is very similar to their later area of work. Students throughout the educational system often get discouraged when they discover that what they are learning in school has no apparent relationship to their every-day lives or future vocational plans.

Point out the possibilities of transfer. Sometimes the two situations are really alike but the students don't see this unless it is pointed out. If we believe that our Sunday school lesson *is* relevant to life outside of the church, we should say so and be able to say why.

Make sure that the original task is well learned. There is evidence that a lot of experience on the original task will increase the likelihood of positive transfer to a subsequent task. This is one reason why NASA would be unlikely to send up an astronaut who had had very limited experience in the simulator.

Make sure that general principles are understood first. A lot of the moral decisions that must be made today are not dealt with specifically in the Scriptures. In some churches, therefore, the older members have decided what is right and wrong for young people and then taught a lot of rules and "thou shalt nots." This kind of learning may have some merit, but such legalism won't be very helpful when a person must by himself make a moral decision about some issue which is not discussed in the Bible or dealt with in the church rule book. The New Testament lays down some broad principles which should guide our behavior. (See Ro. 14:13; 1 Co. 8:9; Gal. 5:13; 1 Pe. 2:21.) If we teach these in the church, the young person has some scriptural guidelines which can apply to any novel situation that he might encounter later. There are some clear-cut rules in the Bible, but a lot of behavior is unique to a given age and situation and it is here that we apply principles, not rules.

Teach the student how to learn on his own. Parents and educators in the twentieth century have a unique problem. Unlike our predecessors who could make a pretty accurate prediction of what life would be like in the future, we can't accurately predict even five years ahead. This makes education especially difficult. The up-to-date knowledge of today may be far surpassed in just a few years. The techniques that a medical student learns today in school might be outdated by the time he completes his internship. *It is of great importance, therefore, that we teach young people how to learn*; how to keep abreast of the changes that will occur as they go through life. Giving them facts is not enough. We must guide as they learn to seek out the information that they need. Sometimes this means showing them how to use a library or concordance. More often it involves asking questions (like "What is the next step in finding out what you want to know?"), giving hints, or providing experience in tracking down the answer to some problem. Perhaps the major task of education—Christian and secular—is to teach the student how to learn on his own.

SPECIAL LEARNING SITUATIONS

Having considered some general principles, let us now look at some specific kinds of learning.

LEARNING WORDS AND IDEAS

A lot of Christian education involves learning the meaning of difficult words such as *faith, trinity, love* or—on a more sophisticated level—*propitiation, sanctification,* and *justification.* To learn the meaning of words, the learner first must come to realize that certain verbal symbols stand for something else. Children discover, for example, that the word *cat* stands for the furry little animal with the whiskers and sharp claws, but it also stands for big tom cats, furry little kittens, Siamese felines and, technically, lions and tigers. In addition, the child must learn how the words are put together grammatically and he must develop the complex skills which enable him to pronounce language clearly and distinctly. With amazing rapidity, most children learn to do all of this, often by observing and imitating others, and frequently in response to the reinforcement that comes in the form of parental praise and delight over the child's increasing communication abilities.

But how can we teach theological concepts and other ideas more effectively? First, we should try to make the idea as meaningful as possible. We do this by giving definitions, using the word in the context of a sentence, giving examples of the term, and sometimes by suggesting a word which is opposite to the one we are trying to define. In Hebrews 11 the writer uses the first three of these techniques to indicate what he means by *faith*. Verse 1 is a definition while the rest of the chapter uses the word in different sentences and gives illustrations. Of course we will have to remember the child's level of understanding as we teach and at times we will want him to use the word in a sentence of his own choosing just so we can be sure that he understands. Second, when a word is used correctly and is apparently understood, the teacher should give reinforcement in the form of praise or encouragement. Third, the order in which material is presented is important. In learning a language, for example, we start with short simple sentences before moving on to something more complex. To arrange subject matter in a sequence that is meaningful to the student is not always easy, however. Some writers have suggested that in our lesson planning we should work backward. Decide what you want the student to know, then work back constantly asking, "What does he need to know *before* he can reach this step?" Fourth, organization is important. Our minds can't handle all of the information that comes our way so sometimes we group facts into more meaningful categories. In learning the books of the Bible, for example, it may be easier and more meaningful if the student can group the books into the Pentateuch, wisdom literature, prophets, gospels, epistles, etc., instead of trying to learn all 66 books *en masse*. The telephone company recognizes this. A person can remember 213-945-6700 much easier than he can recall 2139456700. Fifth, the student should be encouraged to review his learning frequently, and finally, we should try to show how the learned words and ideas can apply outside of the classroom. [15]

LEARNING SKILLS

Learning the meaning of some word is not quite the same as learning how to play the piano, to type, or to knock a little golf ball straight down the fairway. The latter examples refer to the learning of skills. According to the research of one psychologist, [16] this learning occurs in three stages. First the learner thinks a lot about the skill and tries to get the feel of the situation. If he is learning to type or play an instrument, he gets his hands in the proper position and learns how to manipulate the keys or other parts of the instrument. The second stage is the longest. It is here that we consciously refine and sharpen our skills preparing for stage three—the time when we can perform the skill automatically, without consciously thinking much about it. This is how we learn to drive a car. First we sit behind the wheel, get the feel of being in the driver's seat, and take some verbal instruction. Then we learn to operate the car, concentrating on every movement as we do this. Finally driving becomes automatic. We do it often without thinking (a fact which may partially account for the high accident rate).

In teaching skills it is well to remember that people differ in their aptitudes. Some people are "natural" pianists or athletes while others must work harder to develop these skills. For all students, regardless of ability, it is best if the teacher begins by analyzing the skill—breaking it down into parts, describing to the student how it is done and then demonstrating the correct procedure. Also, the student should try the skill while the teacher corrects by telling and showing the learner how to do it better. Then there must be practice in which the learner does the task over and over, gets frequent knowledge about how he is doing, and has the teacher correct ineffective responses. Later

25

the student should also be encouraged to evaluate his own performance so he need not always be dependent on his teacher. [17]

LEARNING ATTITUDES

Some educators have suggested that the learning of attitudes and values may be as important for the child as the learning of facts, information, and skills. To a large extent, whenever a teacher enters the classroom or a pastor steps behind the pulpit, he is showing his attitudes. If he is enthusiastic, compassionate, disinterested, or cynical, the people pick up these attitudes and sometimes adopt them as their own. The teacher who has a real respect for the sovereignty of God, or the authority of the Scriptures will have students who have the same attitudes. Cynical parents or teachers on the other hand, usually have cynical children and students.

To teach attitudes, we must begin by deciding what attitudes we want the child to learn, and then we must make these a part of our own lives. In this way we become an example of what we are trying to teach (see 1 Cor. 11:1). Often we will want to describe the attitudes to the child and encourage or otherwise reinforce him when he shows the attitude in his own behavior.

LEARNING TO SOLVE PROBLEMS

Almost every day of our lives we encounter problems that need to be solved. Because of this, it is important to teach people how to more effectively find solutions to problems. This presents the educator with one of his greatest challenges.

The place to begin is with an understanding of the steps that people go through—consciously or unconsciously—in finding solutions to their problems. First, it is important that we define the problem, attempting to figure out exactly what we have to do and making sure that we have not jumped to the wrong conclusions about the task before us. Then as we keep the problem in mind we start searching for solutions. Sometimes we will consider or even try several solutions and reject each of them before we hit on a solution that works. At other times, our first solution works fine and we need go no further in our search. Basically this is a method of trial and error. Some people are more proficient than others in quickly arriving at a workable solution, depending on past experiences, knowledge, creativity, and expectations. [18] If the problem is "finding a sermon for next Sunday morning," the pastor may go through all of these steps. For some men the solution to this problem is easier than for others.

As he teaches problem solving, the instructor must help his students to identify and spell out the problem that must be solved. Then he must help the students to find and make sense out of pertinent information, and to apply this to the problem. Eventually the various solutions must be evaluated. This is what happens when a professor supervises a student thesis or a parent encourages his child to think. We must be careful, however, to help the student reach his own conclusions without our jumping in and doing it for him.

LEARNING SOCIAL SKILLS

In *Man In Transition* we discussed socialization—learning how to act in ways that are socially appropriate. This is important, not only because it provides for a more harmonious society, but because it gives the child some certainty in life. He learns where he stands and what is required and expected of him.

According to one psychologist, [19] there are several ways by which we teach a child to behave appropriately. First we reinforce behavior which the culture approves. By now the reader will realize that such reinforcement is often in the form of praise, affection, or special recognition of the child's achievements. Second, we create fear, leading the learner to expect that he will be punished or rejected in some way if he doesn't behave. Third, we serve as models, showing the child how he should act. Children have a great tendency to imitate and often they act as if they really are the model whom they admire.

By reinforcing desirable behavior, by not reinforcing and often punishing undesirable behavior, and by being as good a model as possible, the parent or church leader can effectively "train up a child" in the ways of his society.

TEACHING MACHINES AND PROGRAMMED LEARNING

Over forty years ago, a psychologist in Ohio designed a machine that was able to teach, administer tests, and keep track of the student's score. [20] For some reason, this machine never became very popular, but in the 1950s Skinner proposed the idea again and suggested that the teaching machine is an efficient way to apply the established principles of learning to a practical situation. [21]

The earliest teaching machines were very simple. The material to be learned was printed on a long tape, put on rollers and set within a teaching machine which was really a box with a little window on top. Many teaching machines are still of this simple type although more complicated types have also been developed. In one model, for example, information is projected onto a small screen. After the student views the projected information and reads a question about it, he answers by pushing the appropriate button on the face of the unit. If he chooses an incorrect answer, a new image on the screen tells him his answer is incorrect and explains why. Then the student pushes the "return" button, the original question comes back and he chooses another answer. When his answer is correct, the machine advances the film and presents the next piece of information. While simple machines retail for as little as twenty-five dollars (without the program materials) the more complicated models are very expensive, sometimes costing thousands of dollars.

Several years ago it was discovered that the material which was being printed on rolls for a teaching machine could as easily be printed in books. This was a lot cheaper and in most cases just as effective as a machine. Whether it is prepared for a machine or a book, the subject matter in this type of learning is called programmed material, an example of which appears in Figure 1-1. By stopping at this point to complete the program of Figure 1-1, the reader will not only get a feel of what programmed instruction is like, but he will learn about some of the principles that underlie this form of learning.

Skinner once likened programmed instruction to individual tutoring. [22] Both the tutor and the program, Skinner suggested, begin where the pupil is, move at a rate which is consistent with his ability, tell the student immediately if an answer is wrong, encourage him when an answer is right, do not lecture, but instead give hints and ask questions which help the learner to find answers for himself.

Within the past decade, a great deal of research has been done on the effectiveness of teaching machines but the results have not been conclusive. Some studies have found that programmed learning is far superior to classroom teaching while others have found the reverse. [23] Of course just as all teachers are not equally competent, so programs also vary in their quality. It might be expected, therefore, that a good teacher is better than a bad program, and a good program preferable to a bad teacher.

What does all of this have to do with church leaders? In a recent book, [24] Skinner complained that the modern educator (and this would include the Christian educator) does not make much use of the principles of learning which have been discovered by research. The teaching machine and programmed learning was Skinner's solution to this problem. These devices are now widely used in schools, universities, industries, governments, and even counseling centers, [25] but they have not been used much in Christian

29

small	1. Programmed instruction involves several basic principles of learning. One of these, called the principle of small steps, is based on the premise that new information must be present in ____ steps.
small steps	2. The learner gradually acquires more and more information, but always in ____ ____ ____.
active	3. Because active readers generally acquire more knowledge than passive readers, programmed instruction also is based on the principle of active participation. Writing key words as one is reading involves the principle of ____ participation.
active participation	4. While reading the usual textbook, an uninterested learner may slip into a passive state and discover that he cannot recall what he had just "read." In using programmed instruction the learner is prompted to remain alert by writing the key words, thus utilizing the principle of ____ ____.
small steps active participation	5. In these two techniques of programmed instruction; information is presented in ____ ____, and occasionally key words are missing, thus requiring the learner's ____ ____ to complete the statements.
knowledge	6. A third principle, immediate knowledge of results, is illustrated when a professor returns quiz papers to his students at the end of the class in which they were written. These students receive almost immediate ____ of results.
immediate of results	7. If a student makes an incorrect response at any point in programmed instruction, he discovers his mistake because the correct answer may be seen immediately after the frame, before the next one is considered. Thus, in programmed instruction, the learner receives ____ knowledge ____ ____.
immediate knowledge of results	8. Notice that in programmed instruction, unlike the evaluation of term papers, "immediate" does not mean a week or even a day but rather a few seconds. The reader of the program is continuously informed concerning his progress; he receives ____ ____ ____ ____.
small steps active participation immediate knowledge of results	9. Let us review the three techniques of programmed instruction already considered. By means of ____ ____, the reader learns new material, which he acquires through ____ followed by ____.
review	10. At this point, the fourth principle, review, already is apparent to the reader. Since new information may interfere with the recall of previously acquired information, earlier material is periodically repeated in programmed instruction. Thus programming techniques also involve the principle of ____.
small steps active participation immediate knowledge of results review	11. On Sundays many coaches show their players movies of Saturday's game. Each play is seen in slow motion, a procedure which suggests the technique of ____ ____. As the films are shown, various team members are asked to make comments about the plays. The procedure requires ____ on the part of the players. The coaches do not wait until the middle of the next week to show the films because the players profit most from ____ ____ ____ ____. Sometimes the movies are shown two or three times before the next practice and often a single play is rerun several times. This procedure is similar to the programming technique of ____.
small steps active participation immediate knowledge of results review	12. List the four programming techniques below: 1. ____ 2. ____ 3. ____ 4. ____

*Reprinted with permission from N. L. Munn, L. D. Fernald Jr., and P. S. Fernald, *Introduction to Psychology*, Boston: Houghton-Mifflin, 1969, p. 246-47.

education, even though some isolated reports have shown that the facts of Scripture can be taught very effectively by this method. [26] Since material that is studied by programmed learning is remembered longer, and since students and teachers like to learn in this way [27] it is very likely that this technique could be a valuable tool in the church, especially with students who differ widely in ability or interests.

There are some problems however. For one thing, there are very few good Christian education programs and almost none which are consistent with the truths of Scripture. This is due, perhaps, to a lack of interest among many Christian educators and to the difficulty and time involved in designing programs. It has been estimated, for example, that to prepare a good program takes anywhere from fifteen minutes to an hour's work on *each question.* [28] In addition there is the problem of trying to program those parts of Christian education which cannot be broken down into a logical analysis. Because of these difficulties, it may seem wiser to forget programmed instruction and devote our time to something else. In so doing, however, there is always the possibility that we may have pushed aside a very valuable learning technique. Ultimately more research will be needed to determine the extent to which program materials should and can be used in the local church.

REMEMBERING AND FORGETTING

For the educator and student it is a little disconcerting to face the fact that forgetting begins the moment learning ends. This in itself would be discouraging enough but there is also evidence to show that most of our forgetting occurs within a few minutes after learning. By noon on Sunday, most of what was taught during the 9:45 Bible study hour is gone from the brain of the student—perhaps forever.

Why people forget and how they can remember better are topics which have been part of psychology since its beginning. In 1885, a man named Herman Ebbinghaus studied this problem by using nonsense syllables — meaningless combinations of three letters such as JOM, XEY, or LIQ. Freud wrote about forgetting. William James, the man who authored a massive psychology textbook in the early 1900s, studied forgetting in the only experiment that he did during his whole lifetime. Almost every introductory psychology book mentions the problem and a perusal of recent scientific journals shows that the mystery of memory is still a very live issue. [29]

As we study memory, it is important to realize that forgetting is not all bad. Unpleasant ideas, immature thoughts, unimportant details and incorrect ideas are all best forgotten. Most of us would agree, however, that it would be nice if we were better able to keep in mind those ideas that are best not forgotten.

WHY PEOPLE FORGET

For many years it was assumed that forgetting was simply due to disuse. If a path isn't used, the trees and bushes grow over and the path disappears. Likewise, this theory suggested, if an idea isn't used or a skill isn't practiced, it will disappear from our memory. This belief is difficult to prove or disprove but there is growing evidence to suggest that memories do *not* fade with the passage of time. Old people who have difficulty remembering what happened yesterday often show that they can recall very vividly some events from the distant past. In addition, it has been shown that mild electrical currents applied to different parts of the brain can cause a person to recall events and scenes from the past which he had long since forgotten. [30] Apparently memories are stored chemically in the brain and sometimes these memories persist for a long time even though we don't consciously think about them.

In contrast to the disuse theory is a view which holds that forgetting occurs because new ideas come along and interfere with the old. All of us have had this experience at some time. We learn Hebrew and then Greek vocabulary and find that the two get mixed up. We try to remember two phone numbers and find that we can't keep them straight. This is another way of saying that we forget because of the negative transfer that we discussed earlier in the chapter.

Although a memory may be distorted when new ideas come along to interfere, there is also evidence to show that conscious memories can sometimes be wiped out altogether. When a mental patient is given shock treatment he usually forgets all of the events which came immediately before the shock. Emotional shock can have a similar effect. In one experiment, students were asked to learn and then recall a list of nonsense syllables. Partway through the experiment, the back of the chair was made to collapse, an electric shock was felt in the arms, tiny pieces of scrap metal fell from the ceiling, a pistol shot rang out and the room was plunged into darkness. To my knowledge nobody had a heart attack from the shock but there was a large drop in the amount of material that was remembered. [31] The same kind of amnesia has been seen in accident victims who can't remember the details of their accident. It is possible that the shock of the accident interferes with the memory of events which came before, but Freud proposed another theory.

We forget, Freud said, what we want to forget. A car coming right at you on a highway or a shell hitting your arm in battle are very difficult things to think about. As a result the unpleasant details of our injury are pushed out of conscious awareness and forced into the unconscious. Later, under hypnosis or the influence of so called "truth drugs" the memory can come back into conscious awareness, but for a while we forget what we don't want to remember. When we talk about the "good old days," we tend to have unconsciously pushed from our mind all of the memories that weren't so good about the days gone by.

Freud believed that we never really forget anything; we just push from our conscious memory those events that are unimportant or emotionally arousing. As researchers increasingly turn their attention to the physiological aspects of memory they find that Freud was right. Memories may get distorted and interfered with but they rarely disappear from our brains completely.

IMPROVING MEMORY

If we sift through the research on memory and forgetting we can conclude that forgetting is least likely to occur when the learner wants to remember and learns with the intention of remembering; the subject matter is organized, logical, and meaningful (material that makes sense is more easily remembered than nonsense syllables); the subject matter is consistent with the learner's attitudes and beliefs (we tend to forget what we don't believe); the learning is followed by a period of rest or diversion activity (to prevent interference); the learning is reinforced (by pleasant feelings, praise or some other reinforcer); overlearning occurs (which means that we keep studying even after we feel we know the material pretty well); and the learner is not influenced by strong emotion or drugs.

Even when all of these principles are kept in mind, we still forget at times. Three weeks before the final a student studies for the exam and discovers later that he can't remember anything. All is not lost, however, for the student will find that relearning goes much faster than the original learning. In preparing for tests, therefore, it is good to learn the material well in advance and then relearn it and review it as the date for the examination gets nearer.

LEARNING IN THE CHURCH

The hour between 9:45 and 10:45 has been described by some critics as the most wasted hour of the whole week. In some Sunday schools the hour on Sunday *is* a waste, but it human learning. We know, for example, that a desired reinforcement greatly aids and speeds up learning if the reinforcement comes soon after the individual learns. When reinforcement stops, so does behavior, and in most cases learning stops also.

Punishment is an important part of learning. It doesn't stop behavior permanently but its effects last long enough for the learner to discover a better and more acceptable way of behaving.

Our whole goal in education—Christian and secular—is to help the learner acquire information and skills, to remember what is important, and to transfer his new learning from the classroom situation out into the world where he lives. Psychological research has uncovered principles which make learning, transfer, and remembering more effective.

These principles are summarized in this chapter and applied to such practical situations as the learning of words, ideas, skills, attitudes, problem-solving techniques, and social skills. We also discussed how learning principles have been incorporated into machines which are designed to teach.

2

What Causes Behavior: The Psychology of Perception, Emotion and Motivation

O'Hare Terminal in Chicago is reported to be the busiest airport in the world. Everyday, great numbers of planes land on the O'Hare runways, move to discharge cargo or passengers into the giant terminal building, and later take off again. Even people who have grown up in the jet age cannot help but be amazed as these giant aircraft descend from the skies and lift themselves up again bound for almost every part of the world.

If the Wright brothers could visit O'Hare today and look at one of the "jumbo-jets" they might, after recovering from the shock and surprise, want to know how the plane works. A designer or mechanic could show them the various parts of the engines, could point out the dials in the cockpit, could explain the engineering principles that keep the plane aloft, and might even demonstrate how the stewardesses make coffee or bake rolls in the galley. Each of these parts of the plane is important; each must be carefully understood by the aeronautical engineers. In order for flight 168 to make it safely from Chicago to London, all parts of the aircraft must function together in unison.

When we are working with people in the church we are dealing with something far more complex than a giant airplane. Just as the jet has parts which can be understood, so people and their behavior can be studied in fragments. We can look, for example, at the stages of human development, reactions to stress, individual abilities, personality traits, or ways of learning, but we must never lose sight of the fact that a human being is a complex organism in which all of the parts must work together. In this chapter we turn to three very important aspects of human behavior: perception, emotion, and motivation. Together these have a significant bearing on the problems of what causes people to behave as they do and how individuals can be motivated more effectively.

PERCEPTION

At any given time during the course of a day, our bodies are bombarded with literally hundreds of stimulations. The eardrums, for example, constantly respond to noises of all sorts—music on the radio, voices, a ticking clock, traffic outside, or the sound of a neighbor's lawnmower, to name a few. Numerous impulses strike the retinas of the eyes, and our sensitive skin picks up such sensations as the pressure of the clothes on our bodies or the temperature in the room. In addition to these stimulations that come from the world around us, there are also messages from inside the body—like the awareness of a toothache, of hunger, of excitement, of boredom, or of a need to urinate. All the time, even when asleep, our bodies are receiving these messages and doing something with them.

Fortunately all of these messages do not get into our conscious thinking. The complex nervous system is so designed that there is a weeding out process which prevents many sensations from reaching the brain and becoming part of our conscious awareness. Sometimes the incoming stimulations are simply ignored. We don't pay any attention to the sound of a ticking clock, the movement of hair across our foreheads on a windy day or, for some people, the ringing of an alarm clock. It has been estimated that in any one day the average resident of the United States is bombarded with between 650 and 1000 advertising messages [1] but happily (for us, not for the advertisers) most of these are either ignored or immediately forgotten. At other times the body responds automatically to the stimulation. An example is the driver who shifts gears in his car and doesn't give any thought to what he is doing.

When the psychologist talks about perception he is referring to the way in which we respond to these incoming stimulations and hence become aware of the world around and within us. Perception plays a major role whenever we communicate with others, when we witness or counsel, or when two people have a disagreement. It is important, therefore, that the church leader have some understanding of how perception occurs, how it is distorted, and how it is important in the local congregation.

HOW WE PERCEIVE

Figure 2-1 is a highly simplified diagram showing what happens during the course of perception. Both inside and on the surface of our bodies there are millions of nerve endings known as *receptors*. These are sensitive little organs which are able to pick up stimulations from outside of the individual and from inside. The retina or back part of the eye, for example, contains an estimated 125 million receptors, each of which can pick up rays of light and many of which are sensitive to color. When our eyelids are closed and light is not entering the eye, the receptors on the retina may still be active. During dreams, for example, there are numerous eye movements and it is quite possible that the retinas are being stimulated by impulses that originate within the brain. [2]

Once the stimulations are received they pass through the nervous system (along nerve pathways) in the form of electrical impulses. Some of these impulses stimulate muscles and thus influence our behavior before they even get to the brain. If your finger touches a hot stove, for example, you remove it before the message even gets to the brain where you can think about it.

At the base of the brain there is a complicated network of nerve fibers known as the reticular formation. This is the part of the nervous system which keeps us awake and it also plays a great role in helping us to sleep. It is here too that many of the incoming sensory impulses are censored— weeded out so they never make it into our conscious awareness. [3] Even the impulses that do get through are often changed in some way so that what we think we perceive may differ from what really is coming along the nerve pathways.

At this point we might ask why some sensory messages get into conscious awareness while others do not, and why some of the messages get changed. These questions concern the issue of attention.

Attention. If we became consciously aware of every stimulation that the receptors picked up, life would be chaos and we would be overwhelmed by all of the demands on our attention. It is necessary, therefore, that some of the impulses be filtered out. Those that get through to awareness do so either because there is something special about the stimulus itself, or because there is something within the perceiver that lets certain stimuli get into his awareness.

Let us look first at the influence of the stimulus. Advertisers, if they are to be effective, must get and hold the attention of prospective buyers. To do this, they have discovered, there are certain ways in which information can be most effectively presented. Pictures, for example, attract attention better than words (remember what the Chinese said about one picture being equal to a thousand words); pictures with human beings are more attention-getting than pictures without people; a rhyming passage is more attractive than the same passage presented as a narrative; what is on the upper half of a page is more often noticed than what is below, and the left-hand side of the page gets more attention than the right. [4] Then, as most of us are aware, people are more likely to notice what is loud, bright, colorful, mov-

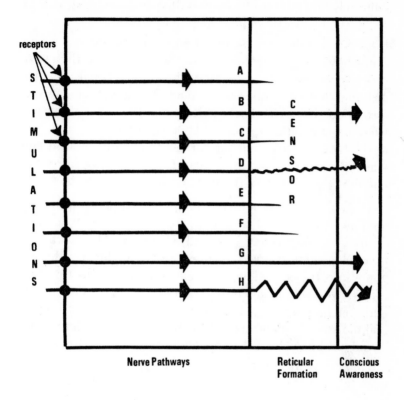

Figure 2-1
How we Perceive.

Stimulations are received by the nerve endings known as receptors and then passed through the nervous system in the
form of electrical impulses. The reticular formation (a part
of the brain) censors the incoming information. Some of the
sensations (such as ACE and F in the figure) are "weeded out"
and never reach conscious awareness, some (D and H) are
changed, and some (B and G) reach conscious awareness un-
changed.

43

ing, large, novel, or repetitious. Writers of television jingles and makers of neon signs are aware of these factors. The church leader who wants to advertise his services or design tracts might keep these principles in mind also.

Even when they are paying attention to the same stimulations, however, all people do not "see" the same things. A well-known illustration describes the architect, artist, geologist, and farmer who look at a field. The architect sees this as a good site for a ranch style home, the artist thinks of what a fine painting this could be, the geologist is interested in the type of rock, and the farmer thinks of the kind and yield of crop that could be planted. Clearly the *interests* and *past experiences* of these men influence what they saw.

This is what psychologists call selective perception—a tendency to look at a situation and see only what we want or are expecting to see. In a study done several years ago a psychologist interviewed a number of job applicants. Before going into the interview, all applicants were told that the interviewer was competent, experienced, and efficient, In addition, half of the applicants were told that he was "warm" and the other half learned that he was "cold." The interviewer did not know what the applicants had been told but after the interview was over almost everybody saw what they had been led to expect, either that he was warm and friendly or that he was cold and aloof. *Expectation*, therefore, influences our attention so that we see what we are expecting to see. A person like Billy Graham might be observed in a rally and seen very differently by his critics and supporters. The former look for and see faults, the latter expect good qualities and this is what they see.

In addition to our interests, past experiences, and expectations, there are other factors which determine what we see. *Emotion* influences perception. If we are very angry, fearful, grief-stricken, or elated, we see things differently than when we are not experiencing these emotions. The phrase "love is blind" recognizes that the lover sees only the good characteristics and is blind to many of the bad or undesirable qualities in his beloved. *Motivation* is another important variable since it is widely recognized that we see what we want or need to see and overlook other things. As we shall see in the next chapter, parents of retarded children see many "signs of progress" that the rest of us don't see. Here is attention in accordance with one's hopes. This also works in reverse—we often fail to see or hear what we don't want to experience and sometimes we unconsciously defend ourselves against anxiety simply by not noticing things that might make us anxious. Finally, there is the matter of *learning*. We all know that snow is white. If we take a colored picture of a snow scene under blue skies, under a setting sun or under clouds, however, we discover that the camera records the snow as being blue, orange, or grey. The surroundings are tinting the landscape, and our eyes—like the camera—really do see the colors; but since we know that snow, in itself, is white, we ignore the hues and see what we expect—whiteness. Here is an example of our brains ignoring the stimulation that is actually being received and seeing, instead, *what we know to be true*. In Figure 2-2 we see the door as being rectangular even though the image that hits our eye is a trapezoid. The man at the right of the figure is probably seen as being closer to us than the door. This is because we have learned that the closer something gets to us the larger it is.

SOCIAL PERCEPTION

Since the stimulus and the observer exert so much influence on what is perceived, it may be wondered if two people ever see the same thing. In all probability the answer is no—two people never do see things *exactly* the same.

Look, for example, at Figure 2-3. Four people, A, B, C, and D, are looking at issue X. Individuals A and B see almost exactly the same thing. They differ from the viewpoint

45

of individual C and everybody differs from D. Notice that C is close to the issue and can see a great deal of it. D on the other hand is far removed and has very little contact with the issue being considered. Now let us assume that issue X is a new choir director. A and B, who might be members of the deacon board, see the man in pretty much the same way. C, who has a more comprehensive and closer view of the man, sees him from a different perspective, while D sees him still differently. Although he may be very vocal in his opinions about whether or not X should have been hired, D is nevertheless far removed from the situation and doesn't have much evidence on which to make a judgment. Notice that the same choir director is seen by all, but each sees him a little differently. In all of this, the choir director also has a view of himself and this may only partially agree with the perceptions of A, B, C, and D.

Figure 2-2
The influence of learning on perception.

The door looks like a rectangle, even though in B and C the image that strikes the eye is a trapezoid. The man looks closer than the door. This is because we have learned that near objects are larger than objects that are farther away.

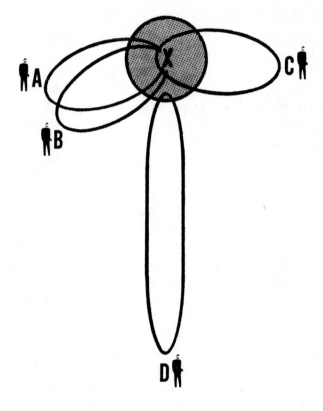

Figure 2-3
Different views of issue or individual x.

Four individuals all see the situation or person differently. See the text for further information.

So much in our behavior is influenced by perception that two psychologists have built a theory around the idea. All behavior, they suggest, without exception, is determined by the individual's view of the world—including himself. Of course, our perceptions change and so does our behavior, but at any given moment a person acts largely in accordance with his view of the world.

PERCEPTION AND THE LOCAL CHURCH

A knowledge of perception can help the church leader in at least three ways. First, in *teaching* we will want to make use of stimulations other than words alone if we really want to have an impact. Our audio-visual aids should be carefully designed to attract attention, but not cluttered up with so much detail that the viewer gets distracted from the message that we are trying to get across. [7] In a Bible geography course, for example, a good colorful map can be a helpful teaching device, but don't leave it up to distract the students when you have gone on to a new topic. Second, in *promotion*, the same principles apply. Many of our advertisements both in the newspapers and on the radio or TV could be better planned. The same could be said for the design of gospel tracts or the covers on Christian books, although recently there have been great improvements in these areas. Even the design and color of a sanctuary can influence the worshippers, as any good architect knows. Third, an understanding of perception helps in our *getting along with people*. When we can learn to recognize that others see things differently than we do and when we try to understand the other person's point of view, then we are certain to get along better. Furthermore, we must watch our own perceptions. What we think we see in another person might not be what's there at all. Perhaps Paul had some of these things in mind when, in his prayer for the Colossians, he said, "We are asking God that you may see things, as it were, from his point of view by being given spiritual insight and understanding"

(Col. 1:10, Phillips). As we come to know Christ better, to be more familiar with His Word and open to the leading of His Holy Spirit, we come more and more to "see things . . . from his point of view."

EMOTION

Following one of the big American political conventions a well-known radio preacher gave a message on emotion. It's acceptable to holler and carry on at political meetings, he said. Enthusiasm, joy, sorrow, and even anger are tolerated at a football game, but let a preacher give even a hint of feeling about his faith and the congregation gets distressed because the pastor is "playing on people's emotions."

Although many people don't like emotion in the church, the fact remains that we are emotional people. Jesus was not afraid to show the feelings which He experienced and other Bible figures talked about their feelings quite openly.

THE MEANING OF EMOTION

Everybody knows what an emotion is but few people can give a very good definition of the term. For purposes of discussion, let us think of emotion in three ways: as a feeling, as a physical reaction, and as a motivator.

Emotion as a feeling. For most people, an emotion is something which we feel or experience—such as anger, love for another person, or amusement because we have heard a good joke. While it is common to assume that "everybody feels just about the same way we do" this is not true. Some people apparently feel emotions very intensely, and thus at times they may be deeply discouraged, extremely worried, wildly excited, or "madly in love." In contrast, others are "not very emotional" at all and don't seem to feel strongly about anything.

Whenever we feel an emotion, we usually express our feelings in some way. Gestures, words, tone of voice, posture, and facial expressions are the most common ways of showing what we feel but, even here, there are individual differences. Little children are spontaneous and very willing to show feeling openly but as we mature we are taught to control emotions and to express them in socially appropriate ways. Some people learn to hide their feelings; others are more open. People in one culture learn to display their feelings differently than do people in another society.

For some of us, one or two emotions may be so predominant that they characterize our whole outlook on life. Every church has people who are always down in the dumps, and others who are consistently enthusiastic or optimistic. Other people are moody. They have one emotion like anger, discouragement, or optimism which persists for several hours or days and influences both their actions and view of the world. (The person who has a "bad mood" is mad at everybody and has difficulty handling normal daily stresses.) Seemingly there are even differences in the emotional tone of whole churches. Some congregations are very reserved and staid. They would cringe if someone cried or said "amen" in a service. At the opposite extreme are churches where there is an abundance of hand-clapping, foot-stamping, and enthusiastic expression of feelings. Depending somewhat on our upbringing, most of us will feel more at home in one emotional climate than in another. Regardless of our preferences for the type of church service, it should be realized that as followers of Christ we must feel some emotion about out faith. Love, joy, peace, sorrow, and even anger over injustice are mentioned frequently in Scripture, but how we express our feelings will depend largely on our upbringing and past experiences. [8]

Emotion as a physical reaction. Whenever a person feels angry, nervous, or other wise emotionally aroused, he frequently is aware of changes in his body. His heart beats a little faster, his muscles feel tense, his breathing rate changes, and he may break out in a sweat or feel unsettled "butterflies" in his stomach. These physical changes, of which we may or may not be conscious, are often accompanied by changes in the chemical composition of the blood, in the normal movements of the stomach and intestines, in blood pressure, and in the activity of brain cells.

These physical changes were studied many years ago by a Canadian psychologist named William Blatz. [9] In an experiment similar to one described in the preceding chapter, Blatz invited eighteen college students to participate in a study of heart action. In a darkened room the subjects were seated in a chair and recording devices were set up to measure heart activity, breathing, and other physical reactions. While the recording was taking place, Blatz pulled a switch which caused the chair to collapse suddenly on a padded floor. All of the subjects reported that they felt momentary fear, and the physiological measures also showed a change. The heart beat and breathing rate, for example, both increased.

In the Blatz experiment the emotion and accompanying physical changes only lasted for a short period of time. Sometimes, however, an emotion such as worry, frustration, or grief persists for a long period and when this happens the accompanying physical arousal persists also. This can lead to ulcers, headaches, high blood pressure, or other emotionally produced illnesses. Drugs, surgery, and other medical procedures can temporarily relieve some of the symptoms of these illnesses, but as long as the emotional tension persists, the illnesses will last also.

It should not be assumed, however, that emotion-produced physical reactions are all bad. On the contrary, the physical changes which are part of emotion often enable us to cope more effectively with the emotional situation. Without the extra physical arousal it would be much more difficult for us to meet and adjust to the crises of life.

Emotion as a motivator. Emotions often arouse us to activity and direct our behavior. The student who is anxious about his performance on a test, for example, is thus motivated to study harder. When we are worried or in love (or both) our behavior is different because of these feelings. At times, however, emotion can have an adverse effect. The actor who forgets his lines because of stage fright, or the students who do poorly on a test because of high anxiety, know that emotion can interfere with effective functioning.

Emotions are so influential in motivating our behavior that some psychologists have even suggested dropping the term "emotion" from psychology textbooks altogether and using the term "motivation" instead. [10] While this is a question for experts to debate, the church leader can recognize that emotion has a powerful influence on how people act. Some public speakers, for example, including evangelists who deliberately try to arouse emotional reactions in their audiences, often discover that this technique does cause behavior to change—people do come down the aisles in response to an emotional approach.

Throughout this series of books we have repeatedly noted the influences of emotion on almost every aspect of human behavior. In human development, for example, fear was seen to be one of the chief ways in which children acquire the norms of society. The child learns when to be afraid and how to both control and express his feelings. In considering memory we noted that intense emotion sometimes causes us to forget—as when we cannot remember what happened immediately before an accident—while at other times a little emotion stimulates us to learn and remember better. Turning to perception, we realize that emotion influences what we see. The young lover or the despondent housewife see things differently because of their emotional state. Our social behavior, which will be discussed in chapter four, is also influenced by emotion (we relate to people differently when we are angry than when we are happy), and so is our thinking and ability to concentrate.

EMOTION AND THE LOCAL CHURCH

Jesus lived in a time when stoicism was a widely-held

doctrine. This was the belief that reason is the highest goal in life and that every man should strive for perfect self-control, to be unmoved by feelings or sentimental considerations.[11] In His teachings and in His behavior, Jesus never accepted this stoic doctrine. He showed love, compassion, anger against sin, and humor.[12] At the grave of Lazarus, Jesus wept and as He approached His own death, He experienced anguish, distress, and loneliness. He spoke of Christian joy, but warned the disciples that the Christian walk could involve difficulties and frustrations.

In view of the teachings and example of Jesus, and in view of the prevalence of emotion in our day-to-day experience, it is surprising that so many people believe that feelings and emotional expression are undesirable, unhealthy, and something which should be repressed. Certainly emotion which is completely out of control can be dangerous. Riots, lynchings, and mob behavior come when emotion is allowed to run rampant. But just as emotion without intellectual control is dangerous, so reason without feeling is unnatural and unhealthy. In the local church and in our personal lives as Christians we must recognize that a complete absence of feeling and an unbridled emotionalism are equally unnatural and unscriptural.

For the church leader, an understanding of the nature of human emotion can have relevance in at least three important situations: in the church service, in interpersonal relationships, and self-understanding.

Emotion in the church service. No writer can state how much emotion should be shown in a service, any more than a football coach can define how the fans should react in the stands. As we indicated previously, people differ in the extent to which they experience and express feelings. Some feel more comfortable in a highly emotional service than do others. Usually, young people are more emotionally outgoing than their grandparents; Pentecostals are more expressive than Episcopalians; blacks are more emotional than whites. What we must avoid are the extremes of cold unemotional rationalism and uncontrolled, emotional fanaticism. The former produces spiritual deadness or lifeless ritualism while the latter often leads to inefficiency, physical exhaustion, shallow theology, and undignified excesses. Church leaders must recognize and avoid the danger of these two extremes, while seeking to hit a midpoint which most effectively meets the spiritual and psychological needs of the individuals in the congregation.

Emotion and interpersonal relations. When we recognize that some people are more expressive than others and that some even feel more deeply than others, then we can be less critical and more accepting of those whose emotional expression differs from our own. In counseling, we must recognize that fear, anxiety, worry, anger, envy, guilt, and discouragement are all present in church members. Instead of criticizing counselees or preaching at them to "snap out of it," we should try to understand the causes of their feelings, helping them to overcome unhealthy emotional experiences or to express feelings in more acceptable ways. This may take time, a lot of discussion, and great patience on the part of the counselor. It may also involve a change in our point of view. If we can see things from the other person's perspective (whether he is a counselee or not), we can often be more understanding when a person shows what we consider to be inappropriate emotional behavior.

Emotion and self-understanding. When we understand something about our own feelings and are able to deal with our emotions, we often get along better with others, feel more at peace with ourselves, and can be more effective in the work to which we have been called.

If emotions are to be a healthy part of our lives we must learn to accept the fact that they exist, we must try to understand them, and we must learn to express them. To do all of this the following guidelines can be helpful both to the church leader and to the members of the congregation.

1. Don't try to ignore emotions. We are emotional people, and to deny our feelings is unhealthy and perhaps not even possible.

2. Try to understand. Self-insight doesn't solve all our problems, but if we have some understanding of our feelings—what causes them and how we are reacting—then we can handle them better.

3. Learn to express feelings. This can be done privately (as when we cry alone) or with a friend (when we talk about our feelings). Sometimes we can even express ourselves by hitting a punching bag or a golf ball.

4. Keep control of your imagination. When we are emotionally aroused, our mind sometimes plays tricks on us so that a situation gets all out of perspective. Get angry with someone, for example, and you will think of all sorts of additional things that are wrong with the other person. We must recognize and guard against this tendency.

5. Maintain a sense of humor. In an informal survey that was done several years ago, something like ninety-five percent of the respondents said that they had a sense of humor. Most of us like to think we can laugh at a situation but few of us really do. Certainly it can be unhealthy to just "laugh our feelings away" but we should also recognize that to use and enjoy humor is often to tone down the influence of more serious emotions.

6. Change the circumstances. Sometimes we can reduce an emotional reaction by changing the situation that is causing the feelings.

7. Commit your emotional life to God. When a believer yields his life to the control of the Holy Spirit, there is a developing of such healthy emotions as love, joy, peace, patience, and self-control (Gal. 5:22-23). At no place in Scripture do we read that becoming a Christian will remove all of our bothersome emotions, but the Holy Spirit can help us to control our feelings and to put them in their proper perspective.

MOTIVATION

Motivation is the study of why people act as they do. Why does one man attend church regularly and another come only occasionally? Why does one child rebel against his Christian background and another accept it enthusiastically? Why does one pastor like to study while another prefers visitation?

For the reader who has read this far, it will be clear that questions such as these have no simple answers; the causes of behavior are often very complex. Even when two people show similar behavior—as when two members attend church regularly—they may do so for very different reasons.

HOW PEOPLE ARE MOTIVATED

In their experimental investigation, psychologists over the years have arrived at several broad explanations to describe how people are motivated.

Instinct. Studies of animals have shown that certain behavior seems to be inborn. Hens always sit on eggs, orioles always build deep, U-shaped nests, the mating behavior in male rats always occurs in the same way, even when the animal has had no chance to observe the behavior of others.

In the early part of this century, many psychologists concluded that much of man's behavior was also instinctive. Great lists of "human instincts"—including such things as liking people, wanting money, boldness, aggressiveness, and hundreds of others—were compiled, reported in psychology books, and memorized by students. The use of instincts to explain human actions did not last long, however. Students of animal behavior began to conclude that instincts were not nearly so common as had been previously assumed. Some psychologists began to doubt whether instincts really existed in people, and it was pointed out that use of the term "instinct" explained nothing. To say that a man takes a wife because he has a "marriage instinct" doesn't really help us to understand much about the man's behavior. The term "instinct" has, therefore, largely dropped out of human psychology, although animal researchers still make use of the term occasionally.

Need reduction. It is common knowledge that hunger, thirst, pain, fatigue, or other physical needs influence our actions. If an animal is in need of food, it seeks about until it can find something to eat so that the need is eliminated. Biological organisms are always responding to physical *needs* which *drive* them to action. This observation has led psychologists to conclude that the satisfaction of biological needs is an important determinant of behavior.

Such an explanation is far too simple to account for complex human behavior, however. Your reasons for reading this book and my purpose in writing it probably have nothing to do with our physiology. It must be recognized, therefore, that men have needs other than those that are biological. In addition to innate needs there are acquired (learned) needs such as the need for success, acceptance, and love.

Several years ago a psychologist named Abraham Maslow identified and arranged men's needs in a pyramid similar to that shown in Figure 2-4. At the base are physical needs. Without their satisfaction we would not survive as a biological organism. Once these needs are being satisfied, we can then be concerned about our safety needs. Then there emerge the needs for belonging and love, for esteem and for self-actualization—the desire in man to become in actual fact what he has the potential to become. Self-actualization, in Maslow's words, is "to become everything that one is capable of becoming." [13] The needs at the base of Maslow's hierarchy are innate, but as we go up the pyramid, we see needs that are acquired. Notice that there is no place here for spiritual influences on behavior and the theory has difficulty accounting for the behavior of people who are more concerned about higher needs (self-esteem, for example) than they are about lower needs (getting enough to eat). It is also possible to criticize Maslow's choice of needs. Other psychologists have different lists and although men undoubtedly have needs that they act to satisfy, it may be that the need-reduction explanation is only a little better than the long-rejected instinct theory of motivation.

Desire for stimulation. At the basis of the need-reduction theory is the idea that people want to have their needs met and their tensions *reduced.* At times, however, people seem to want an *increase* in tension and stimulation. If we simply have to reduce our hunger need periodically, why do some people spend $6.50 on a carefully cooked steak, in preference to a 45¢ hamburger? If we want to satisfy safety needs, why do people go on roller coasters, engage in scuba diving, swallow LSD, or take chances that could easily be avoided? [14]

Apparently in order to survive everybody must experience changing stimulation. There are, however, individual differences in the complexity of stimulation to which we are attracted. What is too simple for an adult may be just right for a child. What is too complex for a beginner may seem simple to an expert. What is a "normal" level of noise for a teenage musician may be too much for his grandmother. [15]

Several years ago some interesting experiments were done at McGill University in Montreal. Student volunteers were paid $20.00 a day to lay on a bed with ears, eyes, and hands covered and with instructions to do nothing. The subjects soon got bored. They sang, whistled, and talked to themselves in an effort to provide stimulation. Before long they became angry, discouraged, and unable to think clearly. These people were *not getting enough changing stimulation* to keep them happy and thinking clearly. [16] At the other extreme, people sometimes get perplexed and inefficient when there is *too much stimulation.*

To use a more familiar example, let us assume that someone is listening to a sermon which is very boring. As the preacher drones on, the listener is not being stimulated

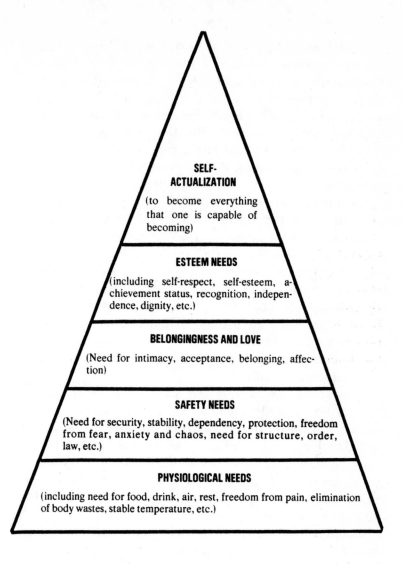

SELF-ACTUALIZATION

(to become everything that one is capable of becoming)

ESTEEM NEEDS

(including self-respect, self-esteem, achievement status, recognition, independence, dignity, etc.)

BELONGINGNESS AND LOVE

(Need for intimacy, acceptance, belonging, affection)

SAFETY NEEDS

(Need for security, stability, dependency, protection, freedom from fear, anxiety and chaos, need for structure, order, law, etc.)

PHYSIOLOGICAL NEEDS

(including need for food, drink, air, rest, freedom from pain, elimination of body wastes, stable temperature, etc.)

Figure 2-4
Maslow's pyramid of human needs.

According to Maslow, human needs are arranged as shown above. Those at the bottom are most urgent and must be satisfied before the person can be concerned about higher levels.

very much so he fidgets, daydreams, and tries to create stimulation in his own mind. On the other hand, if the sermon is exceptionally good—a progression of meaningful ideas—the listener may be overwhelmed as he tries to assimilate all that is being said. Ideally the message should hit some hard-to-define middle point. But this is not easy. What is ideal for a college student might not be ideal for the high schooler or businessman. What is good for one listener may be too complex for some and too simple for others.

When people are in situations which are not very stimulating they look for extra experiences. Although there are various reasons for taking drugs, it is probable that many people want to be "turned on" so that they can experience vivid sensations in place of the dull routine of their ordinary lives. Other people may engage in dangerous sports or daring activities for similar reasons—to find excitement. At the other extreme, when the stimulation is too intense we try to ignore it or avoid it. For some people the stimulation is so intense that their only alternative is to withdraw into a state of schizophrenia.

Unconscious motivation. The satisfaction of needs and the seeking of an ideal amount of complex stimulation do not account for all of our behavior. Sometimes we act in accordance with habits which have been learned or future goals which we are trying to attain. It is also very likely that much of our behavior is caused by unconscious influences. Freud first proposed this idea as a major part of his theory of motivation.

According to Freud, all behavior is motivated, including slips of the tongue, dreams, forgetting, and even accidents. One of the tasks of counseling, according to Freudian theory, is to uncover and help the counselee to become aware of the underlying influences on his behavior. Unconscious motives are difficult to observe and measure, but undoubtedly they do have some influence on our actions.

An alternative explanation. In *Fractured Personalities* we outlined the causes of abnormal behavior and summarized these in a diagram. Figure 2-5 is a similar attempt to summarize the causes of behavior in general. If we want to understand behavior at any point in time, we must be aware of the stimulation which is influencing a person at that moment and we must know something about the person who is behaving. Notice that this explanation makes room for a variety of causes for human behavior; it recognizes that needs, the desire for stimulation, habits, past learning, and unconscious influences might all be significant; it acknowledges that the Holy Spirit and satanic "principalities and powers" can influence men; and it recognizes that the causes of behavior change constantly. Such a diagram will not satisfy those who like clear-cut explanations for the way people act, but concise explanations are rarely accurate and often simplistic—especially in explaining human behavior.

MOTIVATION AND THE CHURCH

The topic of motivation has been studied intensively by psychologists, but most of this work has been done with animals and relatively little has dealt with the practical issues of how people are motivated. The following conclusions are consistent with the conclusions of psychological research that has been done.

People are motivated to engage in activities which satisfy needs. The same students who are bored in class sometimes have an avid desire to read or to work on car engines. Presumably they have needs which are not being met in class, but which are being met in other activities. In one survey of church drop-outs [17] mentioned in chapter four, it was found that many people left the church because it did not satisfy their needs. If their needs are being met in church, people will come. This is another way of making the oft-repeated statement that we have got to be relevant. It should

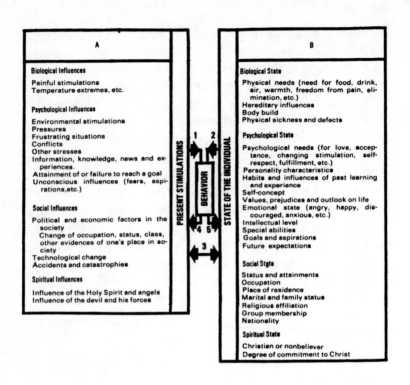

Figure 2-5
The causes of human behavior

There are two main influences that cause behavior: the stimulations which hit the person's sense organs (see box labelled A) and the state of the individual at any given time (see box labelled B). Any one or a combination of the influences listed in box A can cause us to act (arrow 1). A painful stimulation, for example (see the top of the list A), can cause us to jump or to yell "ouch." Likewise, the influence of the devil (see the bottom of the list A) can also cause us to act in certain ways. In addition, any of the states listed in box B could also influence behavior (arrow 2). The need for food, for example (listed in box B under "Biological state"), or the psychological need for love (listed in box B under "Psychological state") can influence our actions. Sometimes the stimulations listed in box A and the states listed in box B influence each other (arrow 3), and often our behavior is caused by forces that come at the same time from both sides of the diagram. The arrows numbered 4 and 5 show that our behavior in turn can affect both the stimulations listed in box A and the states listed in box B.

The items listed in boxes A and B are among the most obvious causes, but they are not necessarily the only influences on behavior.

also be remembered that what is relevant and need-satisfying for one person or age group may be irrelevant for another. Once again the issue of individual differences raises its head.

Incentives are important. An incentive is a desired goal. Sunday schools sometimes give pencils or books to students who learn Bible verses. The pencils and books are incentives for some people, although—as every teacher knows—what is desirable to one person is not an incentive at all to another.

As we saw in the preceeding chapter, an incentive need not always be something tangible. College students often work for a grade or a degree and most of us are willing to work for acclaim. Sometimes the incentive is internal—a feeling of success or achievement, for example—but it takes time and training to instill these values. The Scriptures talk about rewards in heaven, abundant life on earth, the experience of joy and peace—all of which are incentives for the Christian. Every church leader would do well to periodically think about the issue of incentives and to consider how these might be used to motivate people in the church.

The level of changing stimulation is important. It has become a widely-held joke in our society that sermons are dull and that the height of boredom is a Sunday school picnic. In many situations this is undoubtedly an accurate picture. We must remember that young people need more varied stimulation than older people, and that most people in the church need more than they are getting. A college student who is encouraged to think all week won't have much time for a church where he listens to dogmatic assertions and is told not to ask questions. Happily a church which seems to teach the principles of Scripture need not be afraid of stimulating thought and discussion about the Word of God, since truth has nothing to fear from questioning. Many church leaders need to rethink their form of worship and to update and add variety to their church programs in order to make them more stimulating.

People are better motivated when they have a clear goal, when they are given some guidelines in reaching the goal and when they have some expectation of success. In any organization—including the various departments of a church, it is well to ask periodically, "What are we trying to accomplish?" When our goals are unclear, or when we have no idea how to reach the goals that we do have, then we aren't likely to be highly motivated. Even with clear goals and clear strategy, we get discouraged if we can see no chance of success. Sometimes it is best to reach a major goal by setting intermediate but more easily attainable goals. For a college freshman, a Ph.D. is a long way into the future but there are other, more accessible goals—like passing freshman English—that can help a person to reach his ultimate ends.

High stress and anxiety can hinder our motivation. As with learning, so in motivation a little anxiety can help in our behavior, but too much anxiety and stress interfere with motivation.

The Holy Spirit can and does motivate. Every church leader has seen situations where behavior changes noticeably following a conversion experience or the committing of one's life to the Holy Spirit's complete control. The third person of the Trinity moves men (2 Pe. 1:21) and guides them (Jn. 16:13). In his theology, A. H. Strong notes that "we perceive the presence of the Holy Spirit, not by visions or voices, but by the effect he produces within us in the shape of new knowledge, new love . . . new energy." [18] (And we might add, new motivation.)

SUMMARY

For purposes of discussion it is sometimes necessary to look at small segments of behavior, even though we know that in real life all of these segments fit together. In this chapter we have considered perception, emotion, and motivation—all of which have a bearing on the behavior of people in the church.

Perception is the process through which we become aware of the world. At any point in time, our sense organs are being bombarded with hundreds of stimulations, most of which we ignore and many of which we distort to make them consistent with our own interests, past experience, expectations, emotions, motivations, and learning. An understanding of perception is important in Christian education, in the promotion of church activities, and in our relationships with other people. Many of the disagreements between people (in the church and without) occur because we do not perceive things as others do.

Emotions involve both feelings and physical changes within the body. Emotions can motivate us to act more effectively or they can paralyze us so we can't respond at all. For many centuries there have been people who think that the experiences and expression of emotion are bad, but feelings are part of our human nature and certainly should be part of Christian experience. Emotions can get out of control, however, and the church leader must strive to hit a midpoint between the total absence and uncontrolled expression of feelings.

When we study motivation we are considering the question of why people act as they do. The reasons for a person's behavior are highly complex and involve the reduction of needs, the seeking after stimulation, and the satisfaction of unconscious influences. To understand why people behave involves some understanding both of the stimulation that influences a person and of the behaver's current state and characteristics. In the church we must be aware of how people are motivated and attempt to use this knowledge in motivating Christians to be more diligent in their service for Christ.

3

Why People Are Unique: The Psychology of Individual Differences

At some time during his lifetime almost every male in our society (and probably a good many females), has a fascination with electric trains. In rapt attention we like to watch as the master engineer pushes buttons and moves dials which in turn guide the direction and speed of several little locomotives. More recently, interest has shifted to small racing cars which tear around a track in response to the touch of the owner's fingers on a control box.

At times, life might seem simpler if men were like these little trains and cars—mechanical robots, all cast from the same mold, all functioning in a way that can be understood, all controllable from the sidelines. Church business meetings would end a lot sooner if this were so and the man at the controls could have everything the way he wanted. Everybody knows, however, that this is pure fantasy. Men are not all alike; they differ greatly from one another. Even when people are put together into categories ("Students at that school are very intelligent," "The children here are severely retarded," or "Those people are poor losers.") there are large individual differences within the groups.

In casual discussion we often categorize people in terms of their abilities or characteristic traits. We think of a person as being tall or short, introverted or extroverted, honest or dishonest, intelligent or "not so smart." Rarely, however, do people fall into such distinct categories. Very few people, for example, are completely and always considerate and few are consistently inconsiderate; most fall someplace in between.

To illustrate this further, let us assume that we have nothing better to do than to stand on a street corner for a couple of hours and to measure the height of every man who passes. We would probably find that the results of this little experiment would look something like Figure 3-1. In this case, ninety of the men we measured were 69 inches tall, eighty were 68 inches tall, seventy were 70 inches tall, sixty were 71, and so on. If we wish, we could arbitrarily select two points on the scale, say 74 inches and 64 inches, and state that those whose heights are greater than 74 are "tall," while those whose heights are less than 64 are "short." In this way, for the sake of discussion, we have divided our men into three distinct *categories*—tall, medium and short—but we know that there are individual variations within each of these groupings and that the men in fact really are placed along a *scale*. To some readers all of this may seem like meaningless hair splitting but in fact it is a basic consideration underlying all discussions of individual differences.

It should not be assumed that all characteristics are distributed in a bell-shaped curve similar to that of Figure 3-1. Sometimes, for example, there are two or more high points on the curve and sometimes the distribution is "skewed" which means that a majority of people are not clustered in the middle but are towards one of the extremes instead. This is illustrated in Figure 3-2.

To draw curves such as these it is necessary, of course, that we be able to measure the trait that we are studying. Height can be measured with great accuracy and it is possible to get a fairly accurate measure of intelligence. It is much more difficult to measure such things as degree of concern for others, musical aptitude, mechanical ability, or spirituality. Psychological tests have been devised to

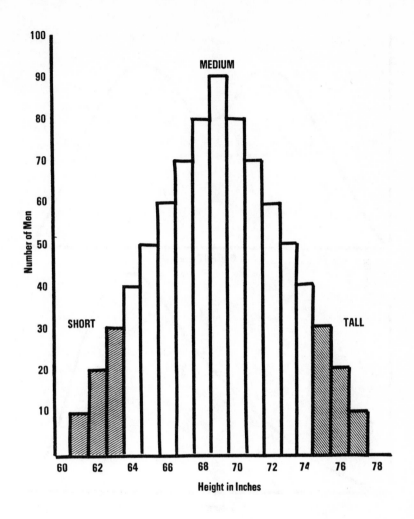

Figure 3-1
Hypothetical distribution of heights.

Very few people are extremely tall or very short.
Most are in between.

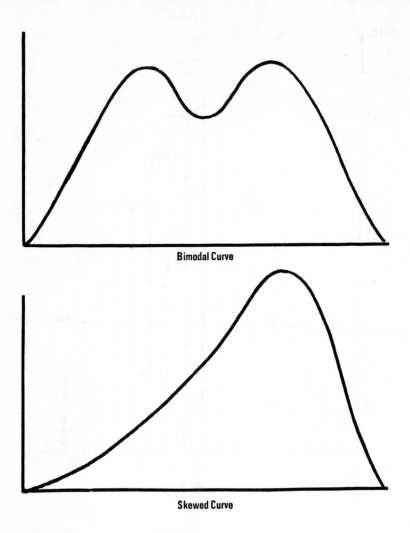

Bimodal Curve

Skewed Curve

Figure 3-2
Commonly observed shapes of curves.

Often a curve has more than one high point as in the bimodal (two high points) curve above. The lower curve is skewed to the right. Here most people cluster toward the extreme on the right of the scale.

70

measure concepts such as these but the accuracy of the tests and hence the accuracy of any curves that might be based on the test results is still in need of further improvement.

THE CAUSES OF INDIVIDUAL DIFFERENCES

With the exception of a few physical characteristics (such as eye and skin color) all human traits are produced by a combination of hereditary and environmental influences. [1] For many years psychologists debated which was more important—heredity or environment—but now we know that both are significant in molding a person and influencing behavior. Even identical twins, who have the same heredity, have different experiences in life and thus are not identical in their interests, values, and outlook on life.

DIFFERENCES IN INTELLECTUAL ABILITY

Several psychological studies, including one on over a thousand children, [2] have shown that intelligence is distributed in a bell-shaped form similar to Figure 3-1. Most people cluster around the middle with an average IQ score of around 100. A few people are so high that they are considered to be in the genius class; others are low enough to be considered mentally retarded.

Sociologists have shown that the choice of a church is determined somewhat by one's social class and wealth [3]— some churches are attended by a lot of rich people, while other congregations are comprised of mostly lower-class and poorer members—but it also appears that churches differ in their intellectual level. College students sometimes discover that the church near campus is attended by a number of professors and other educated people. The sermons and Sunday school class discussions are on a high intellectual plane, far different from the church back home. Both churches may be committed to the Bible as the Word of God (or both churches may reject Scriptural authority)

71

but there is a difference in the intellectual level of the members.

Like most professional teachers and most writers, the church leader must try to plan his messages in such a way that a majority of the people will understand and be stimulated. Hopefully there will be few people, if any, who are too dull to comprehend or too intelligent to be stimulated. Of course to some extent a pastor or youth leader molds the church to his own intellectual level. If a man's messages are "too simple" the more capable people might be inclined to leave and a similar exodus may occur when people can't follow a pastor who is too scholarly and intellectual. Changing churches isn't always easy, however, and many people persist even if they aren't being stimulated. Since it is rarely possible to meet everyone's level, other measures should be taken to meet the special needs of those in the congregation who are highly gifted, and those who are dull. It is here that some understanding of individual differences in intelligence can be important.

THE MENTALLY RETARDED

Let us look first at those who are at the low end of the ability scale. Although mental retardation is defined somewhat arbitrarily, most writers place an IQ of seventy as a dividing point. Anyone whose IQ is seventy or less is considered to be retarded. This group comprises about 3 per cent of the population.

When a person is retarded he is slow in acquiring basic skills such as walking or talking, is unable to progress normally in his school work, and has difficulty in making social adjustment. 4 As an adult, he may not be able to respond appropriately in social conversations, to handle money, or to hold a responsible job. The extent to which one is handicapped in these areas differs from person to person. Table 3-1 shows, for example, that the mildly retarded are capable of functioning quite adequately especially if they are given

Table 3-1

Characteristics of the Mentally Retarded*

Degree of Retardation	I.O. Range	Approximate Per-cent of Total Population	Adult Mental Age**	Characteristics of the Pre-schooler (ages 0-5)	Characteristics of the School Age Person (6-20)	Characteristics of Adults (21 and over)
MILD	50-70	2.80	8-12	Can develop social and communication skills; minimal retardation in sensorimotor areas; is rarely distinguished from normal until later age.	Can learn academic skills to approximately 6th grade level by late teens. Cannot learn general high school subjects. Needs special education particularly at secondary school age levels.	Capable of social and vocational adequacy with proper education and training. Frequently needs supervision and guidance under serious social or economic stress.
MODERATE	35-49	.18	4-7	Can talk or learn to communicate; poor social awareness; fair motor development; can be managed with moderate supervision.	Can learn basic academic skills to approximately 4th grade level by late teens if given special education.	Capable of maintaining himself in unskilled or semi-skilled occupations; needs supervision and guidance when under mild social or economic stress.
SEVERE	20-34	0.12	3	Poor motor development; speech is minimal; generally unable to profit from training in self-help; little or no communication skill.	Can talk or learn to communicate; can be trained in elementary health habits; cannot learn basic academic skills; profits from systematic habit training.	Can contribute partially to self-support under complete supervision; can develop self-protection skills to a minimal useful level in controlled environment.
PROFOUND	Below 20	0.10	2 or less	Gross retardation; minimal capacity for functioning in sensorimotor areas; needs nursing care.	Some motor development present; cannot profit from training in self help; needs total care.	Some motor and speech development; totally incapable of self-maintenance; must have complete care and supervision.

*Adapted from G. W. Kisker, *The Disorganized Personality.*

**This refers to the adults' level of thinking. An adult mental age of 8 means that the adult's thinking is equivalent to that of a 8-year-old child.

73

special training and supervision. They are also able to understand and respond to the love of Christ when churches are concerned enough to include them as part of the local congregation.

The causes of mental retardation. Intellectual impairments result from two major causes: a limited heredity or educational background and a disease or injury. In the first of these, which is sometimes called *mental deficiency*, there is often some defect in the genes that the individual receives at the time of conception. In Down's Syndrome (commonly known as mongolism), for example, there is usually an extra chromosome. In other cases a gene may be defective, or there is an abnormal combination of chromosomes. [5] Even if the genetic makeup is normal, deficiency can still be present if the child has been severely deprived of early educational opportunities. Children who have been neglected or the so-called "wolf boys" that have occasionally been found wandering in a forest someplace, give every appearance of being intellectually below normal—apparently because they have never had the opportunity to learn the things which most children acquire during the formative years.

At conception, some children receive a normal hereditary endowment and then at a time before, during, or shortly after birth they experience disease or brain damage which interfers with their intellectual functioning. This group, known as the *mentally defective* includes such people as the microcephalic who has a very small head and a brain which never fully develops; the hydrocephalic person who has a disease which leads to a great enlargement of the head accompanied by the destruction of brain cells; the cretin whose dwarflike appearance and mental retardation results from a malfunctioning of the glands; or the victim of encephalitis who often experiences a mental deterioration as a result of his disease.

In spite of ongoing research and considerable existing

74

knowledge about mental retardation, it has been reported that in only one out of five cases is it possible to trace any certain cause or causes. [6] A knowledge of what produces the condition, however, is rarely necessary for church members who want to minister to the retarded in their community.

Parents and mental retardation. In *Effective Counseling* we discussed some of the reactions of parents when they have a sick, dying, or physically handicapped child. When the youngster is mentally handicapped the parents' response is much the same. Guilt, self-condemnation, frustration, anger, and the persisting question "Why?" are all present and sometimes made worse by the feeling that mental retardation is really a disgrace. [7]

In working with the parents of retarded children, one chaplain has distinguished between mature and immature responses. [8] Mature responses, those which lead to the best possible future for the child, include an honest acceptance of the fact that the child is retarded and an attempt to set and work toward realistic specific goals. This is not to say that such parents react with a cold stoic determination. Usually they experience great distress when they learn that the child or overprotect him so that he cannot develop appointment, these parents are able to mobilize their energies and to help the youngster as he faces the great frustrations of life.

Immature responses are those which arise because parents cannot bring themselves to face the fact that their child is retarded. These parents cling to the hope that the doctor is mistaken and sometimes they shop around hoping that someone will give a diagnosis and prognosis which are more to their liking. Often there is an attempt to explain away the problem by suggesting, for example, that the school, the child's physical condition or perhaps even his laziness are responsible. In some cases the parents openly reject the child or overprotect him so that he cannot develop even his limited capacities. Frequently the parents feel guilty because of what they might have done to create the situation, and at times there is a tendency to build fantasies and false hopes about what the child will really be able to do at some time in the future.

In working with these parents the church leader must first ponder his own attitudes about retardation. [9] If he is shocked, repulsed, or anxious over the presence of mentally retarded people in the church it is unlikely that he will be very helpful in ministering to either the retarded person or his parents. Often a visit to an institution for the mentally retarded and a chat with the chaplain or other official there can contribute to a healthy attitude toward these people.

Church members are not the only people in the community who are concerned about retardation. The church leader, therefore, must be willing to join forces with local physicians, psychologists, educators, and others as together they work with the children and help the parents to plan realistically for the future. It is only the Christian, however, who can really bring the comfort of the Scriptures and help the family to grapple with the problem of "why." Church members can encourage, give practical aid, and help parents to develop the mature attitudes which will in turn assist the child to live as best he can in spite of his handicap.

The church and mental retardation. In addition to helping the parents, Christians can often have a direct impact on the retarded person himself. Most of these people live in the community, not in institutions, and most are able to learn when they are patiently taught. [10] Christian education for the retarded, therefore, should be a major concern for the local church. If a person is mildly retarded he might be kept in regular classes and given special attention. More often, however, a class might be started for retarded children themselves. Teachers of such pupils should understand something about retardation and be familiar with special techniques that can be used in teaching. [11] The teacher, for example, should use simple language and try to avoid abstract terms such as *faith, hope*, and *charity*. The instructional periods should be short and although physical motion is good there should not be a lot of complicated actions to accompany music. A bright and attractively decorated meeting room is desirable, but too many decorations and pictures can be distracting. Retarded people like things to be fairly rigid in terms of the format, time, and places of meeting. Above all, they require patience. The pace should be slow and there should be no three-point sermons—one point is enough. It is well to remember that regardless of the size of the body the retarded person has the mind of a child. He must be treated as a child—with love, understanding, and patience.

The church that is planning an education program for the retarded might seek the services of a professional teacher who could teach the class. Such teachers are very scarce, however, and even when several churches cooperate in holding a class, it is still difficult to find trained instructors. At such times lay teachers would probably find it helpful to visit a local school and discuss education of the retarded with a professional teacher.

In addition to our programs of Christian education, we can also help the retarded through counseling. This is especially true of teenagers and adults who often lack normal abilities to cope with the frustrations of life. In a counseling relationship, the retarded are usually very dependent and highly suggestible. Because of their limited intellectual ability, such people are also frequently directed by their emotions. The church leader should recognize that these characteristics exist and accept them, but at the same time he should encourage as much independence as possible. [12] In counseling, as in education, cooperation with relatives and others who are working with the retarded is important.

THE INTELLECTUALLY GIFTED

At the other end of the ability scale are those with superior intelligence. In 1921 a psychologist named Lewis Terman began a study of over one thousand of these gifted children all of whom had IQ scores of 135 and above. It was planned that these people would be studied for their whole lives, and at present the project is still continuing even though Terman is no longer living.

In 1970, the "gifted children" reached an average age of sixty. Far from being sickly and poorly adjusted, these people are above average in terms of physical health, mental stability, marriage adjustment, and professional accomplishments. In addition to being highly creative themselves, they have produced offspring who are also intellectually superior and very successful. [13] Apparently there is no support for the theory that the children of capable people are inferior.

Although Terman and his colleagues have focused greatest attention on the male members of the gifted group, others have shown that intellectually superior women are also superior to the less gifted. One recent study of highly competent women psychologists showed, for example, that these women as a group "tend to be more intelligent, socially aloof, dominant, serious, adventuresome, sensitive, flexible, imaginative, insightful, unconventional, secure, and self-sufficient than adult women in the general population . . . and less anxiety prone." [14] It should be added (male readers please forgive me) that these women were also more intelligent and more radical than a comparable group of gifted men.

PROBLEMS OF THE INTELLECTUALLY GIFTED

It should not be assumed that gifted people sail through life without any problems. On the contrary, superior intelligence creates unique challenges for the individual who must grow up and live in a world where almost everyone else is intellectually inferior.

Consider, for example, the problems of being a gifted student. The school curriculum is often too easy and this leads to boredom. The child's superior ability along with the knowledge that may have come from his reading can lead to conflicts with teachers who are less knowledgeable. Because they feel threatened, teachers (and later professors) sometimes ignore or try to stifle the gifted student and to pass him off as a "smart little brat." Because school is of no challenge, superior students sometimes give up. They read a lot on their own but they refuse to do the assignments and soon there are poor grades. In high school they may be "underachievers" and in college they sometimes become "student radicals." Of course not all gifted children react in this way to their boredom. Because they are so capable, most rise above the school situation and succeed in spite of their education.

Non-academic problems also beset the gifted, however. Sometimes parents who recognize the child's abilities set high standards and then exert considerable pressure for the child to succeed. This can lead to rebellion on the part of the young person while at other times it produces "driven people" who are so intent on getting ahead that they never develop smooth relationships with others. Perhaps it is not surprising that in one study over half of the gifted children thought of themselves as being failures. [16]

None of this is meant to contradict the positive picture of the gifted that was presented a page or two back. It appears, however, that for many capable people their success comes "in spite of" as well as "because of" their superior abilities.

THE CHURCH AND THE MENTALLY GIFTED

While educators and psychologists have shown an increasing concern over education of the gifted, church leaders have by and large ignored these people. If the intellectually superior child is bored in school, might he have a similar reaction to church programs that are planned for more average people? Attendance at school is required by law but if the gifted person is bored at church he simply stays away.

While there may be agreement on the importance of meeting the needs of the gifted, it is difficult to know how this is to be done. Research into the problem is continuing and some practical guidelines are already available. According to one report, the teacher of the gifted must teach more, teach rapidly, and teach differently. [17] While there must be emphasis on content, the students should also be taught how to teach themselves. In church, for example, instead of giving pat answers, teachers should show students how to search the Scriptures on their own in pursuit of answers. Young children will appreciate a lot of variety and opportunity for creativity while the older students will want to see how the Bible touches their lives and how Christianity speaks to the practical problems of the day. Obviously, teachers of such groups must take their responsibilities very seriously and prepare fully.

There may have been a time when followers of Christ could remain in a theological ivory tower, ignoring the world around, and dutifully saying "amen" to the pronouncements of the preacher. If such an era ever existed it is now past. Our churches today are filled with thinking people and we must make special efforts to reach their needs. This means that sermons, while firmly based on the Scriptures, must also be intellectually respectable. Special Sunday school classes for the intellectually superior may be advisable but if begun they should be taught by the most capable people in the church. Perhaps the recent trend toward simultaneous "adult electives" in many adult Christian education programs is a more realistic and practical way to meet the needs of the gifted and non-gifted alike. When there are two or more adult Sunday school classes being offered at the same time, one of these can be geared to a more superior intellectual level. The members of the congregation are then free to attend the class which is most challenging to them.

OTHER INDIVIDUAL DIFFERENCES

How do the people in your church differ from one another? If asked to answer that question most of us would probably think of something other than differences in ability. Some people, we might suggest, are very musical while others are not; some are professional men while others don't have much education; some are interested in the youth program of the church while others are more interested in missions; some are always smiling while others are grouchy. These conclusions point to individual differences in aptitude, achievement, interest, and personality. Let us consider each of these in turn since they are all important whenever a group of Christians gets together—in the local church, on a mission station, or elsewhere.

DIFFERENCES IN APTITUDE

When mission societies or governments are selecting candidates for overseas service, an attempt is sometimes made to determine the applicant's language aptitude. Research has supported the widely-held belief that at all ages females are superior to males in word fluency (which means that the fairer sex talks more freely) and ability to comprehend the mechanics or grammar of a language. [18] Even within each of the sexes, however, it appears that some people have a special ability to learn and use languages. Some students can learn a foreign language quickly and with relative ease while others of equal intellectual ability may have a terrific struggle.

The term "aptitude" has been defined as "a capacity to learn readily and to achieve a high level of skill in a specific area." This is another way of saying that an aptitude represents a high potential for acquiring some skill. A person with a mechanical aptitude has a high potential for learning the skills of a mechanic. A person with musical aptitude has a special capacity to detect and recognize such fine points as differences in pitch, loudness, tone, or rhythm. The person with high musical aptitude may not be able to play a note on the piano, but he or she has special potential for being able to do so if given the necessary music lessons. Why people have different aptitudes is a matter for debate. Most psychologists would agree that something inborn contributes to aptitude differences, but of at least equal importance is the influence of childhood experiences.

A knowledge of one's aptitudes can be of importance both in selecting a career and in preparing for further education. Thus far a number of tests have been published which attempt to measure aptitudes, and although the accuracy of many such tests is not good, psychologists are continuing to work at improving their quality.

DIFFERENCES IN ACHIEVEMENT

While an aptitude represents a potential—something which, with training, we *could learn* to do in the future—an achievement refers to some skill or ability that we *have learned* already. When a man hires a new secretary, he wants to be sure that she can type now. If at present she types slowly and with one finger, he isn't very much interested in hiring her, regardless of her potential for becoming a good secretary in the future.

In a church setting, differences in achievement become very important. The man who has attained a degree from a seminary may be more attractive to the pulpit committee than a man who has not had a good theological education. A person who has achieved a reputation for being an excellent speaker may be a better choice for a special series of meetings than a person whose speaking reputation is less established. The music in the morning worship service is likely to be better when the organist has achieved a high degree of proficiency, than when he can do little more than "make a joyful noise."

While it is difficult to get an accurate measure of a person's aptitudes, his achievements are much more easily seen. In churches where there is no bishop to make pastoral appointments, a new pastor is often found by a pulpit committee which has been elected from among the members of the congregation. Sometimes the men and women on this committee will visit another church to hear a man preach without the preacher even knowing that he is being observed. By seeing the man in his own pulpit and by relying on reports from others, it is possible to get an indication of his level of competence as a pastor. Such observations and reports may be biased, but if we ask enough people, an accurate appraisal of a man can usually be obtained.

Just as pastors and musicians differ in their achievements, so if we look into the congregation we are likely to find another great range of skills, achievements, and special abilities. Some church members have an unusually comprehensive knowledge of Scripture or a deep concern for soul winning. Others have a special "way with people" and could do an effective job in visitation. While we must help our people to develop skills in a number of areas, it is also important that we involve people in those areas of the church program where they can most effectively serve. A man whose grammar and education is poor, for example, would be better serving elsewhere than as teacher of the college class.

Although people differ from one another in terms of the things that they can do well, there are also differences in the *range* of abilities. By this we mean that some people seem to have achieved in a number of areas—they can do almost anything—while others are very limited in what they have achieved. There is an understandable tendency to overburden these especially capable people with a lot of work and to ignore the others. Before long a few willing leaders are doing all the work and doing it well while the majority of the congregation sits and watches from the sidelines.

In one of his books, Dr. Elton Trueblood[20] has discussed this in detail. We need to get away from the idea of thousands of Christians sitting in stands watching while a few play on the field. Instead, Trueblood suggests, the local church should be like a team where the pastor serves as a coach and everybody is involved in the action of playing the game. The goal is not to have the coach and his staff carry the ball and play the game alone. The coach tries to get the committed players more active, and the uncommitted into the game. Everybody on the team will not be able or willing to play in the same position. There will be people with different skills playing different roles, but all will be playing to the best of their ability and to the glory of God.

DIFFERENCES IN INTERESTS

While aptitude and achievement have an important influence on the work that a Christian might do, his interests are at least of equal significance. As young children our interests are very diversified and often changing. Because of this we are able to learn much about our complex world. As we grow older, however, this diversity gives way to a smaller number of interests which are more permanent and more intense. Although there are exceptions, it can be generally stated that what we like and dislike in our early twenties we will like and dislike more as we pass through adulthood.[21]

Dr. H. K. Strong, a psychologist who devoted his life to the testing and study of interests, has suggested that interests are learned, that they persist once we get to adulthood and that they differ in their strength (some are stronger than others).[22] In addition, interests influence what we do with our time, what we accept and reject, and how we behave. If my neighbor invites me to go sailing in his boat some evening, for example, I might say no because I am more interested right now in finishing this book. In addition, interests have

84

a great bearing on our choice of work—so much so that vocational guidance counselors make the appraisal of a counselee's interests a top priority part of the counseling sessions.

Often a person's interests, aptitudes, and achievements overlap. This is not surprising since we are usually interested in the things we do best. Sometimes, however, a person is interested in some activity but has no aptitude or achievement in the area. The person who sings off-key but wants to join the choir is an example. The opposite situation is illustrated by an acquaintance of the author's who has outstanding ability as an artist. By every indication he had exceptional aptitude in this area and some of his artwork had won prizes. Everyone expected this man to become an artist but he had no interest in such a career. He wanted to enter business instead and forsook his art for a vocation that interested him much more.

Ideally, the church "head coach" should encourage people to develop their interests. This is of special importance when a person's interests are the same as his aptitudes and abilities. To encourage the development of interests demands flexibility in the church program since creative people are especially inclined to develop and try new ideas. Young people who want a Christian folk music group in the church are likely to be frustrated if they discover that the music which interests them is condemned as satanic but the staid music of their elders is considered "more spiritual." Church leaders who are responsible for planning the programs of specific age groups must be sure that the programs are interesting to the persons involved. To do this, representatives from the age group must help in planning. In spite of their good intentions, a thirty-five-year-old couple cannot, on their own, plan programs which will interest Junior High students or those in the senior citizen's class.

As we seek to develop programs which will be of interest to people within the church, we should also be alert to the interests of those who are outside of the church. According to the Bible, we can expect that nonbelievers will look upon our beliefs as being just a lot of silly nonsense (1 Co. 2:14), but this does not mean that we should throw up our hands in despair and conclude that the unchurched are "just not interested." Instead, our goal must be to catch their interest and to tell them about the love of Christ. While he waited in Athens for the arrival of Silas and Timothy, the apostle Paul talked to a lot of people—Jews in the synagogue, devout persons, passersby in the market place, and highly educated philosophers (Ac. 17:16-18). The Scriptures do not record all of what Paul said but enough is reported to show clearly that the content of his sermons varied with the interests of the people. With the scholars on Mars Hill, Paul talked about their superstitions, but with the religious leaders he reasoned with them out of the Scriptures. Paul recognized that men have different interests and this realization was reflected in his evangelistic appeals. In a more contemporary example, there are dedicated evangelical young people today who recognize that their peers are excited about folk music. As a result, Christian musical groups have been formed which are being used by God to attract the interest of nonbelievers who are coming to Christ in large numbers. Other examples include the establishment of Christian coffee houses, and the attempts by some Christians to penetrate "hippie" communities or student activist groups in order to share the good news of the gospel.

It cannot be too strongly emphasized, however, that to be effective, the programs which are designed to interest the nonbeliever must also be biblically sound. In an attempt to be of interest to the unchurched, we have had a number of theologians advocating everything from sexual promiscuity to civil disobedience. Instead of attracting the unbeliever it is more likely that such radical pronouncements have given an excuse for a lot of uncommitted people to talk their way *out* of the church.23 Looking once again at

Paul we see that while he used different techniques to interest men in the gospel, he did not throw out the gospel in the process. Indeed he had a concern for doctrinal purity and an alertness lest he should fall away himself (1 Co. 9:19-27).

DIFFERENCES IN PERSONALITY

Of all the differences that exist between people in the church, it is probable that personality differences are the most obvious. Some people are always smiling; others are grouchy, or complaining, or friendly, or socially ill-at-ease, or practical jokers. Ask the people in a church to describe what the pastor is like or what the president of the United States is like and you have a rough indication of the personality of these men, of the unique and distinctive characteristics, emotions, abilities, skills, and values which each possesses and displays to others.

Freud and some of his followers concluded many years ago that our basic personality is formed within the first few years of life. Whether or not we agree completely with Freud at this point, it does seem reasonably certain that an individual's personality develops over time and appears to be largely the result of early experiences. As he watches people and interacts with them a child learns how to approach the world and how to relate to others. Some people learn to be suspicious, or friendly, or hypercritical, or sensitive, or stubborn, or concerned about others, or self-centered. By the time we reach the late teens most of us have developed an approach to life which changes very little as we pass through the adult years. This does not mean that an individual's personality is fixed early in life and cannot be changed. Counseling can be effective in helping people to alter their personalities and all of us can work at developing different characteristics. Of great importance in this is the influence of the Holy Spirit. When a life is put under his control a lot of our former traits give way to be slowly replaced by love, patience, goodness, gentleness, and other desirable characteristics (Gal. 5:19-24).

Our personalities have a great bearing on the decisions which we make in life. In choosing a mate, for example, we try to find someone whose personality is compatible with ours. The choice of a vocation may be influenced more by our personality than by our interests and abilities. [24] Even the choosing of a church is influenced by our personality. Although there may be no differences in doctrine, some churches are formal in their worship services while others are very informal. Some congregations are very critical of everyone else while others are very tolerant. Some churches are known to be very friendly to strangers while others have a reputation for being unfriendly and cold. In selecting a place to worship, people are likely to settle on a church which best fits their own personality and for some this may even be more important than the church's doctrine.

The church leader must recognize that these personality differences exist, not only between churches but between members of the congregation. Instead of trying to mold everyone to be like himself, the leader should try to accept the differences and help people to find areas of service that are most consistent with their personal characteristics. When there are traits which others find offensive—such as moodiness or a highly critical attitude—counseling can be effective in helping people to change and to develop behavior which is more appropriate for a Christian.

CONCLUSION

In the early church some Christians apparently failed to recognize the importance of individual differences so the apostle Paul discussed this in three of his letters—Romans (12:6-8), 1 Corinthians (12) and Ephesians (4:8-12). We are all parts of the body of Christ, he pointed out, but we are all different. We have different abilities, different responsibilities, and different areas of service. J. B. Phillips puts this into language which is especially clear:

Men have different gifts, but it is the same Spirit who gives them. There are different ways of serving God, but it is the same Lord who is served. God works through different men in different ways, but it is the same God who achieves his purposes through them all. Each man is given his gift by the Spirit that he may use it for the common good (1 Co. 12: 4-7).

To put it in a more contemporary form of speech, each of us is responsible for "doing his own thing." Our special gift or gifts will be revealed by God and each of us should use these in His service. Since these characteristics are, in fact, gifts from God we should not boast about what we have or envy those who have something that we don't possess.

Clearly, God never intended men to be mechanical robots. We are all different, as modern psychology has effectively demonstrated, and our task as Christians is to work together as one body. This is a difficult task but the Scriptures imply that it is a goal which can and must be reached.

SUMMARY

When we think about people we sometimes pigeonhole them into categories and talk about the introverted, the extroverted, the intelligent, or the retarded. While this categorizing of people can be convenient for purposes of discussion we must realize that all of us are different. We may be similar to each other but no two of us are exactly the same.

When we use psychological tests to measure individual differences, we find that people can be placed somewhere along a scale. In terms of intelligence, for example, a few people—the retarded—are clustered at the low end of the scale and a few extremely intelligent people are at the upper end. The rest of us fall somewhere in between. What is true of intelligence is also true of differences in aptitude, achievement, interests, and personality.

Although some of our differences stem from hereditary

influences, many others are the result of learning and early experience. By the time we reach adulthood many of our differences are well established but this does not mean that change is impossible. An individual's own efforts, the help of a counselor, and the influence of the Holy Spirit can all bring about changes, especially in our interests and personality characteristics.

Church leaders, and church members as well, must recognize that individual differences exist. We should encourage people, therefore, to serve Christ as best they can with the abilities and unique characteristics that they possess. Each person in the church should be willing to serve in the area of his special gifts and while this may lead to some tensions and misunderstandings at times, we should seek to work together as a body, serving Christ as the Scriptures have commanded.

4

When People Meet:
The Psychology of Interpersonal Relations

Man is a social creature whose whole life is spent in the presence of other people. It is almost impossible for him to live completely alone, even if he wants to be a hermit, but at times it is also pretty difficult for him to live harmoniously with others. Many of the major problems facing today's world—war, over-population, pollution, crime, civil disobedience, the demands of militant minorities—result from the inability of people to get along with each other. Even within the church Christians often have difficulty working together. In the Bible, there is an emphasis on the individual and his relationship to God, but we are also told repeatedly to be concerned about our fellow men and to live together in peace and harmony. The church leader, therefore, must be concerned about such social issues as cooperation among people, the nature of leadership, prejudice, the influence of rumor, and the ways in which people communicate. These topics have all been studied by social psychologists and it is to these and related issues that we now turn.

SOCIAL ORGANIZATION

In years gone by, political visionaries used to talk about all men being equal, about a classless society where everyone would have similar wealth, status, and opportunity. In theory this sounded good, especially to the oppressed, but in practice it is unlikely that there can ever be a society where everyone is equal. Some people will always have greater wealth, education, skill, or ability than others. As a result, some people will be more important to the group and because of this they will get extra attention, acclaim, and responsibility. Whenever people get together, someone soon emerges as a leader, an initiator of action, and thus a person of higher status. Every society, therefore, and every large group of people within the society is in some way organized. Sometimes the organization is clear to everyone—as in the military where each person wears a uniform to indicate his rank in the group—but more often the social organization is less obvious.

In attempting to understand how groups are organized social psychologists frequently make reference to status and roles. The term *status* refers to the position that one has in a social group. In a government, the president or prime minister usually has the most important and influential position. We say, therefore, that he has the highest status. The cabinet members have a lower status and the civil servants are even lower.

To some extent, our status is determined at the time of birth. In many societies men have a higher status than women, whites have a higher status than blacks, and people who are born into respected families have a higher status because of the social position of their parents. Unlike some eastern countries, status in the West depends less on our birth than on what we have achieved or accomplished. Hence the doctor, the highly educated individual, or the athletic star are given special recognition because of what they have done in life.

Whether we want to or not, all of us give out signals to show our status to other people. The military uniform which we mentioned above, is a clear "status symbol" but we can advertise ourselves in other more subtle ways. Our occupation, the kind of car we drive, the size and location of our home, the style of our clothes, and even the words we use in conversation are among the signs which give evidence of our status. So important is this that some people buy bigger cars, install swimming pools, or purchase color TV sets (whether they want these or not) simply because possession of these things gives the appearance of high status. This in turn gives the individual a feeling that he is important and a person of worth. By convincing others of their importance, many people are able in turn to convince themselves.

In some parts of the world it is quite difficult to change one's status, but in the West (and especially in the United States) it appears that people can improve their place in the society. As a result, we have been branded as a nation of status seekers [1] in which people are striving to keep up with, and when possible, to surpass the Jones'.

A *social role* is the kind of behavior that the society expects from a person with a given position or status. We expect that a national leader will be more dignified than, say, a laborer, or that a college professor will be more interested in academic matters than will a truck driver. If a member of congress turns out to be an undignified playboy, or if the college teacher prefers "turning on" with drugs instead of studying books, we are surprised because the person has not behaved in accordance with the role that we expected.

We need not be prominent personages to play roles however. All of us play a variety of roles every day. A Sunday school teacher, for example, will act differently when he is in the classroom, when at a teachers' meeting, when on vacation, when stopped by a policeman for speeding, or when playing ball with his son. As he takes on different roles, his behavior changes accordingly. From the time of birth all of us learn how to act in socially appropriate ways— which is another way of saying that we learn how to act in accordance with our various roles in society.

In spite of its declining popularity, the church is still an important social institution in our society. From a strictly human perspective, the local church provides recreation and social fellowship, teaches values, is an agency for helping people who are distressed, gives meaning in confused times, and is a vehicle through which society can be changed. In the opinion of some people membership in a church conveys respectability, while for others the church provides a place for acquiring status and prestige, or an opportunity to participate in colorful pageantry.[2] More recently, churches have become centers for sensitivity training or political action and forums for intellectual debate and discussion.

When we turn to the Bible we see that the local church was meant to be more than a social institution. The members may come from different geographical areas, religious backgrounds, and occupational groups, but having invited Christ to control their lives,* they all become one in the sight of God (Gal. 3:26-29; Col. 3:11). In one sense, therefore, the church has potential for being the only one-class institution in the society. All of its members are alike before God—redeemed because God has given them a new life (Eph. 2:8-22).

This is not to imply, however, that believers are all to act in the same way. Some church members have abilities that others lack (Ro. 12:4-8; 1 Co. 12:4-11; Eph. 4:8, 11-12) and it is probable that some people should have more responsible positions (Ac. 6:1-7). This is no cause for gloating however, since every position is of equal importance in the eyes of God (1 Co. 12:14-31) and every man is given the task that God chooses to give (1 Co. 12:18).

---

*In the Biblical record, church membership was not to be granted to everyone who came in the door, but only those who had been saved—to those who believe that Christ is now alive and Lord (Acts 4:47; 16:30-31; Romans 10:9).

Like the congregation in Corinth, people today forget the biblical ideal of believers each fulfilling unique roles and working together in harmony with others and for the glory of God. We still try to impress each other with our status symbols and church leaders are tempted to compete for positions of greater and greater prestige. This can lead to interpersonal conflict within the congregation and to a diversion from the various tasks to which we have been called by God. The church leader should be aware of this natural human tendency for people to strive for status—even within the church. He should realize that as an institution the church can meet many social needs, but he should beware lest the local congregation become *solely* a recreational center, a vehicle for the personal ambitions of its members, a center for intellectual stimulation, or a launching pad for political reform.

GROUPS IN THE CHURCH

When two or more people are in contact with each other and pursuing some common goal or interest, we have a group. While social psychologists might disagree over the question of whether a Sunday morning congregation is really a group, all would recognize that within the church there are a number of smaller collections of people that do fit the group definition. The choir, the church board, each Sunday school class, the women's missionary society, the prayer cells, the youth fellowships—all are examples of groups within the church. While small groups such as these have probably existed since the beginning of the church, we are now in the midst of what one writer has called a "small group explosion." [3] More and more church members are meeting together for sharing, prayer, and study of the Scriptures.

Groups can be of different types. Some are formal with a constitution and elected officers, while others are informal like the morning coffee klatch of a group of housewives. Some groups are exclusive with rigid membership standards,

95

while others are open to anyone. Some groups show a lot of cohesion and permanence, while others are less cohesive and more likely to disintegrate quickly.

While groups have been studied in great detail, we will limit our discussion to three aspects: how groups are formed, how they can be made to work effectively, and why they disintegrate.

THE FORMATION OF GROUPS

Some groups are formed only after a lot of careful deliberation, while others seem to arise spontaneously, perhaps because the members have similar needs, goals, interests, or feelings of attraction for one another. These spontaneous groups arise with little or no prior planning, but it takes more effort to deliberately start a group.

In the first place, if a group is to be deliberately formed and maintained, it must have some clear purpose. Within the church, some groups exist in order to accomplish a specific task like providing music for the worship service, planning the Christian education program, raising money for foreign missionaries, or witnessing to the saving power of Christ. Other church groups are formed for the purpose of studying the Scriptures or contemporary issues. Groups that exist for the personal and spiritual growth of the members form a third category. In these groups, people share experiences, discuss personal problems or concerns, and learn to relate more effectively to others. Included in this category are groups that exist for the purpose of recreation and fellowship. Fourth, there are prayer groups. Of course many church groups exist for the purpose of fulfilling two or more of these functions simultaneously. [4]

Even if the church leader sees the purpose for a group, he must convince the prospective members. They must come to accept the fact that the purpose is important and—if the group is to persist—they should also be in on the discussion of when the group will meet, for how long, and what its members will do. To be effective, members will have to agree to give of their time and energies to the group since it is probably true that a group which asks nothing of its members can expect little in return.[5] Depending on the type of group, there should be some discussion of organization, whether or not there will be a designated leader, and the extent to which he will lead. All of this may take considerable time before the members begin to work for the purposes that brought them together. When church groups have no clear purpose, have no real organization, and make no demands on the members, the groups are likely to be dead and ineffective. Regretfully, there seem to be many such groups in the church today.

THE DEVELOPMENT AND EFFECTIVE FUNCTIONING OF GROUPS

Once a group gets started, we should periodically try to evaluate whether and to what extent the group is accomplishing its purpose. It can also be profitable to look at how the members are relating to each other as persons.

Group maturation. It appears, for example, that regardless of the purpose for existing, successful groups go through distinct stages of development. Some writers have referred to this as a maturation process and identified the five stages that are summarized in Table 4-1. Once the group and its leader are able to get past the first three of these stages, it can move quickly to maturity and to a maximum efficiency. Too often, however, people in groups prefer to remain in the stage of dependency with the leader making all of the decisions, and the members doing little or nothing. Even when a group reaches the most productive stage, a crisis will sometimes cause a return to stage one and a repeat of the cycle.

Group cohesion. In some groups, the members feel attracted to one another. They enjoy being together and find many opportunities for meeting. These groups are said to have a high level of cohesion.[6] Since highly cohesive

Table 4-1
Stages in Group Maturation*

Stage	Characteristics of Group
Dependence	Group is assembled, has a specified purpose but waits for the leader to make decisions and tell the group what to do next.
Resistance to Freedom	Group feels uncomfortable if they are left on their own. They are anxious, very critical of the leader, and inwilling to take responsibility.
Adolescent Rebellion	Recognizing its responsibility, the group moves to establish operative procedures. Often there is a struggle as members subtly and unconciously vie with one another for prominence. The original leader must expect the criticism and not react with defensiveness or an attempt to keep the group dependent on him again.
Independence	Group "feels good." There is an atmosphere of happy feelings and good will.
Interdependence	The group settles down to productive work. There is less competition and a willingness to work together on issues. The original leader is now respected but accepted as an equal.

*Adapted from W. G. Bennis and H. A. Shepard, "Theory of Group Development", *Human Relations* 9 (1956): p. 415-437; and C. Reid, *Groups Alive—Church alive.*

groups get along well and tend to be productive, it is desirable to have these kinds of groups in the church. But this is not always easy to arrange. If the group is dependent upon the leadership of some authority, or if the members feel that they have little in common with each other, then the group is not likely to be very cohesive, although sometimes a common problem will draw people together and they will work in harmony toward their goal, in spite of individual differences.

Within recent years, ecumenical church leaders have been distressed at the lack of real cohesion among prospective participants in church unions. With time some greater cohesion may come, but this is unlikely if ecumenical unions are proposed mostly by church leaders, if the church members feel that they have no similarity with people in other denominations, or if the laymen can see no real reason for union. Evangelicals who accept the authority of the Scriptures and are interested in uniting for common evangelistic efforts would seem to have a firmer basis for interdenominational cohesion. Regretfully, these efforts are undermined by a few church leaders who like to emphasize petty differences and turn us into warring factions. To be against some other group or some person can build cohesion within a group (as when the British rallied together against Hitler during World War II), but intergroup conflict, as we shall see shortly, is draining on the people involved and apart from defeat or weakening of the enemy, little else is accomplished. Certainly the cause of Christ is not advanced by denominational smugness and a tendency to be at war with the brethren.

Group morale, The term *morale* refers to a feeling of confidence and optimism about the group and its activities. It is well known that morale and cohesiveness are closely related; if one of these is present, the other is likely to be in evidence also. High morale comes when there is confidence in the group's leadership, a feeling that the group is making progress toward its goal, and a feeling of oneness with other group members. As might be expected, groups with high morale are more productive than groups with low morale.[7]

One of the significant issues facing church leaders today is the problem of low morale. Young people, especially those who are well-educated, are leaving the church in droves. The reasons for this are complex and have been discussed in detail by several authors,[8] but doubtless morale plays a significant role in this exodus. Many young people feel that the church leadership is rigid and outdated, that the church is not accomplishing anything, that the members are divided, and that the church goals are vague. As a result the morale is low. Since there is often little feeling of confidence in the organized church, people are ignoring the church altogether or forming little worship groups of their own.

> Confronted with revolutionary challenges of a changing social order, the institutional church projects, by and large, an image of reactionary stagnation. The horizons of the church are all too often petty and parochial. There is little attempt to play a role which is excitingly creative and fruitfully imaginative in relation to the problems of society. Too often the church reflects rather than reforms the life of society; too often the church is content passively to follow rather than courageously to challenge. Far from projecting an image of self-sacrificing activity, the church, all too often, projects an image of entrenched privilege and smug indifference.[9]

The church leadership and the members must work together to change the circumstances that give rise to such an image. Until we do, there will be a continuation of low morale among many who are presently in the church and possibly an increase in the number who are leaving—frustrated, discouraged, and dissatisfied.

Group conformity. When they watch their children go off to school and later to college, many parents are concerned about how these young people will be influenced by their friends. Such a concern stems from the widely accepted belief that when people become members of a group, they often conform to the standards of the group. If our children "get in with a good group" we are relieved because we believe that the group influence will be good; if the children "get in with a bad group" we are concerned about the effect that this will have.

Research clearly supports this belief in the tendency of people to yield to group standards. There are individual differences to be sure, but for most people the group exerts a powerful pressure for its members to conform. Several years ago, a psychologist named Solomon Asch [10] devised some ingenious experiments to study this problem. In one of these experiments a group of college students was seated in a room around a large table. Let us assume that you are one of these students and are seated at the end of the table. The experimenter shows the group a card on which are painted two lines, one of which is obviously shorter than the other. The assignment is simple since all you have to do is tell which is longer—the line on the right or the line on the left. You clearly see that the line on the left is longer, but one by one the other students around the table announce that in their view the longer line is on the right. When it comes your turn to respond how will you react? Will you say what you think—even though everyone else disagrees— or will you go along with the group? Unknown to you, all of the members of the group are working with the experimenter and all are being paid to give the *wrong* answer. The researchers want to know how *you* will react to the pressure of the group.

In repeated experiments of this type it was found that only about one person in four repeatedly resisted the group pressure and stood up for what he thought was right. Even when people suspected that they were being manipulated, many went along with the group anyway. When other studies

101

investigated opinions, attitudes, and beliefs it was found that these also could be changed by group pressure and that for many people the changed attitude persisted for months after the experiment. [11]

Whether or not a person will conform to the group in his behavior and thinking depends on the significance of the issue (Many of us would have a second cup of coffee because everyone else is doing this, but fewer would yield to group pressure to smoke marijuana.); on the importance of the group that is exerting the pressure (One's close friends are likely to be more influential than casual acquaintances, and we are more likely to yield to a group which we consider to be important.); on the length of time during which the pressure exists (Interrogators know that with persistent pressure, people who resist initially can eventually be "broken down."); on the size of the group (Asch found, as we might expect, that a person was more likely to yield when he was pressured by five or more persons than when he was pressured by fewer people.); on the unanimity of the pressure (If everyone is against you it is hard to resist; resistance is much easier when you have at least one ally.); and on the status of the group members (We are more likely to yield if we think that the other group members have a higher status than our own.) Later in this chapter we will consider how group pressure can be resisted, but at present we should recognize that such pressures are powerful and that they can be both for the benefit and the harm of the group member.*

---

*In a recent significant article, one writer has shown how groups sometimes struggle so hard to maintain a spirit of consensus that they ignore all dissent and disagreement, This tendency to appear united at all costs has been called "groupthink." It occurs in governments and possibly in church groups as well. According to the article, "the more amiability and *esprit de corps* there is among the members of a policy-making ingroup, the greater the danger that independent critical thinking will be replaced by groupthink, which is likely to result in irrational dehumanizing actions directed against outgroups." See I. L. Janis, "Groupthink," *Psychology Today* 5 (Nov, 1971): pp. 43-46, 74-76.

GROUP DISINTEGRATION

Old soldiers never die, it has been said, they just fade away. Old groups sometimes fade away and disintegrate too, but at other times they fall apart because of battles and disagreements between factions within. In the first volume of this series we listed some of the signs which indicate that a group is falling apart. [12] When there is a decline in the feeling of group cohesion, a breakdown in organization, a problem with communication, and a loss of commonly accepted goals, then the group is unstable and in danger of falling apart.

There are a number of reasons why a group disintegrates. Sometimes the purpose for which the group originally formed has been accomplished so the members have no further need to meet together. The campaign workers of a political candidate, for example, may go their separate ways after election day (especially if the candidate lost). Sometimes the original purpose remains unaccomplished, but the members drift away because they are frustrated by their lack of success, no longer interested in the original goals, or more interested in some other activity or group. All of this has been seen in church groups where members leave because of discouragement or declining interest. Another problem may be clashing personalities and factions within the group. Domineering leadership, rigid and inflexible group members, the presence of internal cliques, the tendency of some self-centered people to use the group to advance their own status or prestige, and even the attempt of well-meaning persons to avoid any controversy or appearance of disagreement—all of these can spell doom for a group. For the church leader who wants to keep a group together it is important to be aware of all these influences and to try, when possible, to help the group members to avoid such dangers.

When the people in the early church had disagreements they discussed the situation openly, tried to see each other's point of view, worked together at resolving their differences, and sought the guidance of the Holy Spirit as they moved ahead with their work and service. The same guidelines apply to groups of Christians today. Periodically we must also reevaluate the purpose of groups within the church and resist the tendency to keep some of our groups together just for the sake of tradition. A group that is held together by habit but has no real purpose for existing any longer is already a dead group. In many cases our work would be more efficient if such groups were terminated.

Prejudice, Discrimination, and Conflict Between Groups

When there is conflict between internal factions, the group is in danger of collapsing, but the situation may be different when the group is in conflict with another group. In team sports, for example, if team A and team B are each united behind their respective coaches and determined to win over the other, then the game is likely to be exciting and the team morale will be high. Let one of the teams split into factions, however, and it is hard to muster an enthusiastic offensive against the outside opposition.

Some social historians have suggested that in the 1930s Hitler directed attention to the supposed atrocities of the Jews in order to unite the German nation against a common "enemy" and to prevent the citizens from arguing among themselves over domestic economic problems or the blunders of their leader. On a much smaller level one gets the impression that a few church leaders today use the same tactic. Instead of fighting "the good fight of faith," showing "righteousness, godliness, faith, love, patience (and) meekness" (1 Tim. 6:11-12), they fight other groups of Christians. The Bible does not suggest that we can be united with nonbelievers (2 Co. 6:14) but it does urge followers of Christ to live together in peace and harmony (2 Co. 13:11, Living Letters). When born-again believers unite to do battle with other believers who happen to be in another evangelical denomination or aligned with some other seminary, then we are distracted from our purpose of fulfilling the great commission.

Why do groups come into conflict with each other? By now it will be recognized that there can be no simple answer to this question, but we can consider some of the more obvious influences. One of these is the problem of *prejudice*.

Defined somewhat formally, prejudice is an irrational attitude which leads us to think, feel, perceive, and act in a biased way toward some individual or group of people. [13] Sometimes our prejudices are favorable so that we like the other, while at other times our prejudices are unfavorable. It is the latter that leads to conflict between groups.

Usually a prejudice develops because of the instruction and example of parents and teachers, or because of unpleasant experiences with one or more members of the group against which we are now prejudiced. Returning again to prewar Germany we can see that by criticizing the Jews, Hitler was able to (a) find some helpless group whom he could blame for his own problems, (b) find a group whom he could persecute in order to give release to his frustrations, and (c) feed his own ego by finding a group over which he could feel superior. The behavior of the Ku Klux Klan and other highly prejudiced groups may be explained by some of the same principles. [14]

Once a prejudice develops it influences our further perception. If we decide that all old men are bad drivers, then whenever we see an older male at the wheel of a car we look for bad driving. If we see something bad our prejudice is confirmed; if we don't see something bad we conclude that "that fellow is just the exception that proves the rule."

Frequently, prejudice (which you will remember is an attitude) also leads to *discrimination*. This term refers to *acts* of behavior that arise because of our prejudice. If a person is prejudiced that all people of a given race are dirty, then in his actions he avoids such people and perhaps ridicules them because of their supposed uncleanliness. Often we can tell that someone is prejudiced by watching his actions. Many of us have met people who say, "I'm not prejudiced against blacks," and who may really believe this, but if we watch the person's actions in the presence of black people, we discover that discrimination *is* present. Since it is unlikely that we can ever have discrimination without prejudice, a person's real attitude is displayed by his actions.

Prejudice and discrimination are almost always at the basis of group conflict. If the prejudice is not present before the conflict, it arises as a result of the disagreement. When a group feels that its existence or work is threatened by another, conflict and the accompanying prejudice and discrimination are likely to be more intense.

How this tension can be reduced is a problem which has baffled the most brilliant minds for centuries. Undoubtedly education helps (learning about the other group) and so does the experience of meeting and learning to communicate with the opposition group. Since groups are composed of people it seems likely that there must also be changes in individual men before there can be changes in group behavior. But Christians, who are new creatures because of their commitment to Christ (2 Co. 5:17), have not demonstrated to the world that they have any special abilities to get along. Instead, some research has shown that churches even stimulate prejudice and intergroup conflict. [15]

It should be realized, however, that non-Christian researchers rarely know the difference between a man who attends church and calls himself a Christian and a man who has invited Christ into his life and sincerely desires to be controlled by the Holy Spirit. When church members are divided between those who attend for selfish reasons (to get status, business contacts, relief from guilt, and other personal benefits) and those who attend because they are sincerely interested in religion and want to grow spiritually, the former are highly prejudiced while the latter are remarkably free from prejudice and discrimination. [16] Undoubtedly the latter group is also more likely to be Christian in the biblical sense. This is not to say that evangelical Christians are free from prejudice—many are very prejudiced—but if an individual sincerely wants to abide by the Scriptures he cannot accept Galatians 3:28 and still harbor grudges against minority groups.

The church leader, it would seem, has a Christian responsibility to break down prejudices not only against blacks or Jews, but against liberals, Catholics, or other religious groups with whom we might disagree. The church leader also has a responsibility to avoid stimulating and building up prejudices against other groups. Since prejudices so often begin in childhood and become stronger as the person grows up, it is especially important that we try to help children to avoid prejudices and discrimination. [17] Certainly it is right to speak against nonbiblical doctrine and injustice, but it would be well to remember that while Christ condemned sin, he loved and gave Himself for sinners (Jn. 3:16; 1 Tim. 1:15). By building walls of prejudice between our own little group and everyone else, we cut ourselves off from any evangelistic outreach and show the world that we are "narrow fighting fundies" rather than followers of the living Christ.

OPINIONS, ATTITUDES, AND VALUES

To say that an individual or group has a prejudice is not very complimentary. "Prejudice" and "discrimination" are words which convey a lot of emotional feeling in our society, and the feeling is one of anger and criticism. Rarely will a person admit to being prejudiced himself, and when we accuse others of having a prejudice we are usually describing something of which we disapprove.

In contrast, the words "opinion," "attitudes," and "values"

are much more highly regarded. People like to air their opinions, and newspapers all over the country give frequent reports showing the results of the latest opinion polls. An attitude can be thought of as something desirable and we like to think that we have clear-cut values.

In spite of the feelings which accompany the use of these terms they mean much the same thing. A prejudice and an attitude can be used interchangeably. Both are beliefs or tendencies which lead us to think, feel, see, or act in a certain way towards some person, group, or object. An opinion is also a belief about some person, object, or issue but unlike attitudes and prejudices which can be highly emotional, opinions are strictly intellectual. Values are collections of attitudes and prejudices. All of these terms refer to something which is learned, which influences behavior and which can be measured.

In 1948, when the polls incorrectly predicted that Harry Truman would lose the presidential election in the United States, researchers were forced to take a closer look at their survey techniques. Soon it was discovered that in order to measure attitudes and opinions accurately, the survey questions must be very carefully designed and the respondents must be selected in a way that gives a good cross section of opinion. When the National Sunday School Association sponsored a survey of 3000 evangelical Protestant teenagers, the researchers spent many hours in selecting and wording the questions, getting the questionnaires to large and diversified groups of young people, and carefully analyzing the data. [18] As a result, the findings gave a concise summary of the thinking of young people in the church, and this information in turn was helpful to many church leaders in planning subsequent church programs.

Within recent years, psychologists have become very interested in how attitudes are formed, maintained, and changed, but psychologists are not the only people who are interested in this topic. Advertisers, businessmen, political activists, educators, parents, and many others are concerned about influencing the opinions and attitudes of other people. This is also of concern to church leaders because the great commission involves, among other things, the changing of people's attitudes and opinions about Christ and His teachings. This leads us to the topic of persuasion.

PERSUASION

Changing existing attitudes and guiding people into new opinions and beliefs is really a problem of persuasion. For the church leader, this topic presents two problems. First, we want to persuade men to follow Christ. This means convincing the unbeliever that he should become a Christian and arousing the believer to greater devotion and more diligent service. Secondly, we want to help people to resist the persuasive arguments of those who would attack and seek to undermine the truths of Christianity.

THE PSYCHOLOGY OF PERSUASION

When Paul stood in the presence of King Agrippa and "almost persuaded" him to become a Christian (Ac. 26:28), the apostle was surely aware that it is the Holy Spirit who convicts men of their sin (Jn. 16:8) and leads them to accept the truth (Jn. 16:13). But Paul knew that the Spirit often works through committed men (Ro. 8:14). As ambassadors for Christ (2 Co. 5:20), therefore, who have been commanded to make disciples of all nations (Mt. 28:19-20) we, like Paul, must seek to be guided by the Holy Spirit and at the same time to be as persuasive as possible.

At first glance, it might seem easy to persuade people to forsake their former beliefs and to accept something better. In practice, however, persuasion is usually a very difficult task. People are often hesitant about giving up their long-held opinions and attitudes. Our behavior is largely dependent on these attitudes and thus to change our way of looking at the world is, as we noted in an earlier chapter, to change our whole way of doing things—and most of us are reluctant to do this. Furthermore, people have learned to resist persuasive messages. With so many advertisers who want us to change, we automatically "turn off" the commercials and refuse to give much serious heed to the persuader's appeals. Then there is the matter of individual differences. Some people are, in general, more persuasible than others, and the persuasive techniques that work with one person may fail completely with someone else. [19] Paul apparently recognized this when he decided to use different approaches with different people in order that he might persuade some (1 Co. 9:20-22).

Table 4-2 summarizes many of the persuasion techniques that research studies have shown to be effective. If he decides to make use of these, the church leader must be alert to certain ethical principles. In spite of His foreknowledge, God gave men the freedom to accept or reject Him and thus *in our enthusiasm to convince we must not coerce* or force a man to make a decision against his will. As we seek to persuade men, we must sincerely desire to be led by the Holy Spirit and we must respect the right of each person to make his own decisions.

RESISTANCE TO PERSUASION

After he had completed five years of research on the psychology of persuasion, a well-known psychologist recently concluded that it is "now within man's power to alter experimentally another person's basic values, and to control the direction of the change".[20] Such a conclusion is surely distressing when we realize that the world is filled with people who are actively trying to manipulate others through the use of persuasive arguments, Critics of Christianity and those who advocate other systems of belief are also concerned about persuasion and their arguments sometimes are effective in wooing those who have previously bowed to Christ. Parents and church leaders are often concerned, for exam-

Table 4-2

Some Established Principles of Persuasion*

1. Before changes in attitudes, values, or behavior can occur, the person must be made to feel that his current beliefs are incorrect or inconsistent.
2. When trying to persuade another individual or group, if the audience is friendly, it is acceptable to present one side of the argument; when they are unfriendly, present both sides.
3. When opposite views are presented one after another, it is best to present the one you want them to accept (a) *first* in order when the material is novel and (b) *last* in order when the issue is something with which they have been previously acquainted.
4. For more intelligent respondents* you should let them draw their own conclusions; for the less intelligent it is best to state your conclusions concisely.
5. Intelligent respondents tend to be more persuaded by logical arguments; the less intelligent respond more often to emotional appeals and dogmatic statements.
6. Arousing fear may cause a temporary change, but for more permanent change it seems best to use a moderate amount of anxiety—not too much and not too little.
7. The persuasive message should be introduced along with information and views which are already accepted by the respondent.
8. A person's attitudes and opinions are strongly influenced by the group to which he belongs. People are more likely to be persuaded by persons whom they see as "just like me," or by members of their own peer groups. In general, the closer one feels to a group or the more one wants to belong to a group, the less he is willing to deviate from the group standards.
9. Opinions and attitudes which we hold publicly are less likely to change than those which we hold privately.
10. People are more often influenced by persuaders who are considered to be expert and trustworthy. The message is less likely to be accepted if the persuader is considered to be unethical, a publicity seeker, a professional persuader, or more interested in himself than in the respondent.
11. The successful persuader takes into consideration the respondent's needs, intelligence, and personality characteristics.
12. Repetition of a persuasive communication over a period of time helps the convert to persist in his opinion.
13. A decision is more likely to persist if the respondent must follow his decision to change with some active response.

* The respondent is the person who receives the message, the person whom we hope to persuade.

* Adapted from M. Karlins and H. I. Abelson, *Persuasion*; R. L. Rasnow and E. J. Robinson, *Experiments in Persuasion*; and M. Rokeach, "Persuasion That Persists," *Psychology Today* 5 (Sept. 1971): 68-71, 92.

ple, about impressionable young people who come under the influence of professors and fellow students who are militantly anti-Christian. The problem of how people resist persuasion, therefore, becomes important to those in the church.

Beliefs are often like animals that have been raised in a germfree incubator. As long as the belief is kept in a protected environment where it is free from threat, there is little likelihood that it will die. When subjected to attack, however, the belief or attitude becomes extremely vulnerable. If we want to build resistance, therefore, we must innoculate by exposing the person to a weak dose of the attacking material—a dose that is strong enough to build up his defenses but not strong enough to overwhelm him. There is now a considerable amount of research which supports this conclusion. [21]

The problem spiritually is how to innoculate. Returning to our medical example, we know that an injection which would effectively protect one person may kill another. The physician looks at his patient's physical build, therefore, and adjusts the size of the dose accordingly. Regretfully, in the church we have no such guideline about how much of an innoculation to give and furthermore, we usually must innoculate a whole group at once—in a class. This increases the danger that some might be overcome. Such is the problem for educators in Christian colleges. When they hear non-Christian views presented in class there is always the danger that some students will be persuaded and will reject their Christian teachings even while they are in a Christian college sitting under the influence of a Christian teacher. Rather than risk this, some parents and colleges try to keep young people protected from all non-Christian influences. The young Christian thus becomes like a greenhouse plant, strong and well-rooted so long as he is protected from the world. If he ever gets any idea about talking to nonbelievers, however (like Jesus and Paul did), or winning men to Christ (as the great commission commanded), then the greenhouse Christian is sure to hear some persuasive arguments against his faith. Often this is like exposing an immature sapling to a hurricane. The naive young person is just about that vulnerable.

Each parent and each teacher must decide for himself therefore, how he will innoculate to prevent this collapse. In deciding, it is helpful to remember the following research conclusion about resistance to persuasion. People are less likely to yield when they have been warned that attack is coming; when the warning comes from a person whose integrity and knowledge is respected; when arguments are given to support what we believe and why; when arguments *against* our beliefs are summarized and then refuted clearly; when the immunization goes on for a period of time and doesn't all come at once; and when there are friends and people of higher status who accept the original position (an evangelical professor in a secular college can have a tremendous impact, just by being evangelical). All of these conclusions are based on laboratory studies and surveys using nonreligious material, [22] but some creative researcher needs to study this question using evangelical students. There is danger in this, of course, but the resulting conclusions may be worth the risk.

COMMUNICATION

Many, perhaps most, of the problems that divide people arise and persist because of our inability to communicate. Husbands and wives, young people and their elders on different sides of the generation gap, labor and management, diplomats facing each other at the conference table—all are faced with the need to communicate accurately and to understand the other person's message. Unlike animals, people can communicate using words that have clear meanings and technical devices such as microphones or telephone lines, but these cannot guarantee that successful communication will occur.

To understand why communication so often breaks down,

we must have some idea of what happens when people try to communicate. First, *the idea must be formed* in the communicator's brain. If the communicator's thinking is clear—that is, if he knows what he wants to communicate—then the communication is off to a good start. If the original thinking is unclear, communication cannot possibly be effective. Secondly, *the message must be coded*—put into symbols that will be sent to the receiver (the person with whom we are trying to communicate). Usually we put our message into words, but we also convey quite a lot in a nonverbal way. If he can't find the right words to express his idea, if he uses poor grammar, or if he says one thing with words but conveys something else in his nonverbal gestures, then the communicator fails because his message has not been coded effectively. Third, *the message must be transmitted*. To speak clearly and audibly or to write legibly is important for getting the message across. This will insure that *receipt of the message by the receiver* is accurate. Assuming that he receives the symbols without error, the receiver then must decode and understand the message. This is the fifth step and involves *translating of the words and other symbols into some kind of meaning*. Breakdowns in communication often occur here. If we hear someone speak in a foreign language, we have no understanding of the symbols so we cannot make sense of the message. Even within the same language there can be misunderstanding. For the communicator, the word *father* may mean "someone kind and helpful," but to the receiver, *father* may mean "someone harsh and unloving." To say that "My pastor was like a father to me" may, therefore, mean one thing to the communicator, but to the receiver this means something quite different.

Once the message gets from the brain of the sender to the brain of the receiver, the process is reversed. The receiver becomes a communicator sending a message back to the original communicator. Since messages can be verbal as well as nonverbal, this two-way exchange of information occurs simultaneously. As one person talks the other nods his head, or shows by his facial expression that he understands. Of course at any stage in this complicated process, communication may break down, and this leads to misunderstanding and confusion.

The church leader, like everyone else, must be concerned about accurate communication. Preaching, teaching, witnessing, counseling, participating in a business meeting, getting along with one's spouse, raising children—each involves communication with others; each can suffer when communication breaks down. Because such communication failures are so common, each of us must strive actively to communicate clearly and to understand what others are trying to say. The church leader is also in a position to help other people communicate more effectively among themselves and with God. This must surely be a vital part of our ministry.

LEADERSHIP

This book and the ones preceeding have been written for religious leaders. We frequently have mentioned the responsibilities and duties of those who hold leadership positions in the church. As we approach the end of the series it is fitting that we should turn to a discussion of leadership itself—what effective leaders are like and how they act.

THE QUALITIES OF LEADERSHIP

Several research studies have sought to discover if there are unique personality traits which characterize successful leaders. Summarizing these studies, one report concluded that good leaders tended to be spontaneous, vigorous, sensitive to the needs of others, objective, and high in self-esteem. [23] Later research demonstrated that leaders are highly intelligent, emotionally stable, and able to resist group pressures. [24] Still another study concluded that successful leaders tend to be of two types—the "task specialist" who is able to solve problems and the "social specialist" who is well liked but less able to get things done. It is very rare to find both of these qualities in one person, the researcher concluded, but sometimes the task specialist and social specialist will team up in dual leadership. [25]

Based on studies such as these, most writers now conclude that there is no such thing as a "born leader"—a person who possesses certain traits that will enable him to rise to a position of leadership regardless of the circumstances. Instead, it appears that whether or not a person becomes a leader will depend on a combination of his personality characteristics, his abilities, his status and, (of great importance) the needs of the group. [26] A pastor, for example, is automatically assumed to be a leader since leadership is part of the pastor's job. Whether or not he will be a good leader, however, will depend to a large extent on his personality and his ability to meet the needs of his congregation.

While there are no born leaders, there *is* a tendency for the people who lead in one situation to be successful leaders elsewhere. This is because the skills, attitudes, and ways of thinking which a leader develops carry over to new situations. When he enters a new group such a person acts in leaderlike ways and this, in turn, often gets him into leadership positions. [27] For the person who wants to be a better leader himself, therefore, or for those who want to train others to be leaders, it is important to identify the behavior which successful leaders exhibit.

THE FUNCTIONS OF LEADERS

The person who is an effective leader is first of all a *model* who by his own behavior shows others how to act. This is true not only of the general who leads armies into battle, but of the parent or teacher who wants to lead young people or the pastor who wants to lead his congregation. Closely related is the role of the leader as a *participant*. The leader who stands on the sidelines giving directions is far less effective than the man who works along as a member of the group. One study showed that leaders who participated in the work along with their people saw better morale and more success in solving problems than did nonparticipating leaders. Third, effective leaders are those who show *concern* and interest in group members. Military leaders who appear on the battle lines with their men are showing all three of these characteristics—and so are pastors who take their laymen with them when making pastoral calls. [28]

It should not be assumed, of course, that all good leaders act in the same way. The kind of leadership behavior that is needed in one situation may not be needed in another. According to the findings of one social psychologist [29] leaders may fulfill any combination of the following roles: *administrator*, which involves planning, managing, coordinating, and directing a group towards the accomplishment of some goal; *bureaucrat*, which involves the carrying out of programs that for the most part have been set by others; *expert*, which means being a specialist and resource person in some specific technical area; *ideologist*, which involves the ability to come up with creative ideas; and *charismatic personality*, which involves the possession of characteristics which strongly appeal to others. Some successful leaders play only one or two of these roles; others are more varied in their leadership behavior.

The way in which a person leads will affect the whole atmosphere of a group. In a classic study which was done many years ago and repeated later, [30] groups were subjected to three types of leadership: *laissez-faire*, authoritarian, and democratic. In *laissez-faire* leadership, the groups were given complete freedom to do anything they wished. In contrast, the authoritarian leaders set rigid rules, dictated policies, and criticized those who deviated. The democratic leader called for a discussion of goals and guided the group as they reached a consensus about their procedure. The *laissez-faire* groups accomplished almost nothing and the morale was low. The authoritarian group got a lot done so long as the leader was present, but when he left, the group relaxed and stopped working. Sometimes these groups developed apathy or resistance to the leadership. The democratic groups, on the other hand, worked consistently and efficiently whether the leader was present or not. They showed high morale and much less hostility towards the leader. Some readers might be reluctant to accept these findings since they are so much in line with western political ideology. The studies were carefully conducted; however, and the repetition of the findings in later research adds to the credibility of the results. The church leader who wants to develop efficient behavior and high morale in the congregation would be well advised to forsake the *laissez-faire* and authoritarian types of leadership and—where this can be done—lead in a more democratic manner.

SUMMARY

If he really wants to understand human behavior, the church leader must realize that man is a social being. He is born into a family, grows up in a society, learns to fulfill a variety of cultural roles, and is taught how to act appropriately in a great number of social situations. Sometimes men get along with each other but at other times they argue and perhaps fight.

The entire society is organized into groups, classes, and status positions. Within this organization is the church which itself is organized. Although all believers are one in Christ Jesus, there are differences in the responsibilities, capabilities, and interest shown by the church members. Often the church is organized into smaller groups—the board, the committees, the Sunday school classes, and so on—each of which has a leader and further organization. When new groups form, they often develop and mature like people before there can be really effective work accomplishments. Groups differ in the morale of the members, the extent to which the participants conform to group standards, and the closeness of the members to each other. Some groups, within the church and without, become scorned as objects of prejudice or discrimination and at times there are conflicts between different groups.

Since the church leader must work with groups of people, it is helpful if he can understand how groups form and function. He should know how attitudes are formed and how people can be persuaded to change. Equally important is an appreciation of the ways in which people can learn to resist persuasive arguments, and an understanding of how they can more effectively communicate. This chapter has considered all of these topics and concluded with discussion of an issue that must concern any church leader: the nature of leadership itself.

5

Where Psychology and Christianity Meet: The Psychology of Religion

Psychology and Christianity both seek to understand man and his behavior. Both desire to know the truth; both seek to assist man with his problems and help him to change. But so different are the presuppositions and methods of these two systems of thought that considerable disagreements and tensions have built up between them. In the opinion of one writer, "Psychology and the social sciences are today occupying the center of the stage in the conflict between science and religious faith—a position occupied by astronomy in the 17th century, physics in the 18th, and biology and physical anthropology in the 19th." [1] The same psychology which has enormous potential for aiding the church leader in his work can also present arguments which seem to demolish the church's message and weaken the faith of its adherents. Thus, any honest study of psychology and the church must consider the threats that come from psychological science as well as the benefits. Clearly an understanding of these issues can be of help to the church leader as he seeks to teach and counsel with those who encounter the anti-Christian arguments of contemporary secular psychology.

While the areas of agreement between psychology and Christianity can be succinctly stated, the disagreements are complex and much more difficult to discuss in a short space. This, however, will be our task in the present chapter: a summary of the issues which cause psychologists and theologians to be both friends and foes.

THE PROBLEM OF DEFINITION

In the first volume of this series psychology was defined as a science, and an art, which studies behavior—both that which is directly observable, and that which is less observable. The stated purpose of psychology is to understand, predict, and control behavior.

A concise definition of Christianity is much more difficult. The term "Christian" is traditionally applied to a broad group of people including those of differing and sometimes conflicting theological persuasion: Roman Catholics (with all of their diversity), Jehovah's Witnesses, Eastern Orthodox, Fundamentalists, Christian Scientists, Evangelicals, Liberals, and "death of God" theologians to name a few. There are also many people who have no particular interest in religion but consider themselves to be "Christian" because they live in a country where "Christianity" in its various forms is the dominant religion. All who call themselves "Christians," therefore, will *not agree* with the following definition, but all readers have a right to *be aware of* the meaning of Christianity as used by the author.

In the pages which follow, Christianity refers to a system of belief which is based on the teachings of Jesus Christ and the writers of the Bible. The essentials of Christianity include acceptance of (1) the Bible as the divinely inspired, inerrant Word of God and the ultimate authority on all matters of doctrine and standards of behavior; (2) God as almighty, perfect, and existing in three persons—Father, Son, and Holy Spirit; (3) Man as a divinely-created being who voluntarily sinned and in so doing, alienated himself from God; (4) Jesus Christ as the Son of God who died in order to make man's salvation possible; (5) the physical resurrection of Christ from the dead; (6) the belief that a confession of sin and acknowledgement of Christ as Lord is the only way for

122

man to receive the gift of eternal salvation and to be restored to fellowship with God; and (7) the expectation that Christ will return at some future time to judge all men, to punish unbelievers, and to live forever with believers.

THE PROBLEM OF LANGUAGE

When an Englishman and a Frenchman do not understand each other's language, there are likely to be problems of communication. These problems are easily overcome, however, if a man who is bilingual translates one language into another. *Man* and *homme*, *book* and *livre*, *you* and *vous*, *I don't know* and *je ne sais pas*, are pairs of words which mean the same thing. The two languages use different sounds and grammar to express similar ideas and to define similar objects.

When theologians and psychologists desire to communicate, there is also a language problem. The language of theology is very different from the terms which are commonly used in psychology, and people who are familiar with both fields have tried to translate. Some have equated Freud's "id" with the "sinful nature of man," or "abnormal behavior" with "sin," but such translation is never really accurate. These pairs of terms do not mean the same thing. Psychological concepts such as "ego," "conditioning," or "depression" have no exact equivalent meaning in theology. Likewise, theological and Biblical words like "mind," "soul," and "spirit" are psychologically meaningless. When a Christian tries to describe abnormal behavior or emotional experience in theological terms, or when psychological language is used to describe conversion, there is sure to be oversimplification and inaccuracy.

In order to describe behavior with precision, the science of psychology has developed a technical language which seeks to be specific and unambiguous. The student learns this language, but it is often meaningless to people who have not studied psychology. In like manner, the Bible uses terms to describe spiritual matters. Christians learn what these terms mean, but the unbeliever does not and cannot fully understand (1 Co. 2:14). While the trained psychologist who is also a believer comprehends both languages, he realizes the futility of translating from one to the other or of reducing both to a less (or more) technical level. In spite of these problems, and at the risk of misunderstanding or oversimplification, the following paragraphs will attempt to deal with complicated terminology and issues in as clear a manner as possible.

AREAS OF AGREEMENT

There are at least seven areas where Christianity and psychology are in agreement. Both agree that:

1. *Man has value.*

In the psychologist's opinion, man in and of himself, is a worthwhile creature. The Christian believes that man is valuable because he is God's creation. Although man sinned, God valued (loved) him enough to make provision for his salvation (Jn. 3:16).

2. *Behavior is influenced by various forces.*

Both psychology and Christian theology agree, for example, that behavior can be influenced by biological and social influences.

3. *Childhood experiences have an effect on adult behavior.*

Freud first developed this idea in psychology; the Bible makes reference to it in Proverbs 22:6 and elsewhere.

4. *Man has problems.*

5. *The causes of man's problems can be understood, at least partially.*

6. *Man's problems can be reduced.*

Christianity and psychology disagree on what causes man's difficulties, and there is further disagreement concerning the ways in which these problems can be tackled. Nevertheless, both believe that something can be done to improve society and the condition of individual men.

7. *To change man for the better is a desirable goal.*

PRESUPPOSITIONS

Like any system of thought, Christianity and psychology are each built on some foundational presuppositions. As shown in Table 5-1, there is conflict between the basic pre-assumptions of Christianity and psychology and because of this the two systems are often in disagreement. Let us look at each of these conflicting presuppositions in more detail.

THE WORLD VIEW

Psychology, in accordance with other sciences, presupposes naturalism, while Christianity works on theistic assumptions. The naturalistic view believes that man is alone and sovereign in the universe. He is free to determine his own destiny and to select his own values. Psychologist Erich Fromm has expressed this view clearly. Man, he wrote, "must accept the responsibility for himself . . . . There is no meaning to life except the meaning man gives his life by the unfolding of his powers . . . . [Man is alone] in a universe indifferent to his fate . . . there is no power transcending him which can solve his problems for him." [2]

The Christian theistic position, in contrast, holds that there is a God who exists, who created the world, holds it together, and who influences men's lives (Col. 1:16-17; Heb. 1:1-3). God is sovereign, not man. God's will is the very cause of man's existence and freedom.

DETERMINISM

This is the most basic assumption in psychology. Determinism is the belief that everything which happens, all of the world's processes, are strictly and invariably determined by natural laws. All events in nature including man's behavior, are caused or determined by a preceding event. In making his observations, conducting his experiments,

Table 5-1

The Most Common Presuppositions of Psychology and Christianity

Presupposition	Psychology	Christianity
The World View	Naturalism: man is on his own.	Theism: God is in control.
Determinism	All behavior is determined in accordance with natural laws.	Some behavior is determined, but God and man can freely intervene to influence behavior.
Man's Nature	Man is basically good and capable of improvement.	Man is by nature sinful, although God has provided a way by which man can be changed.
Ethics	All moral choices are relative. Right and wrong depend on the individual and/or the cultural situation, and period of history in which he lives. There is no absolute standard.	Some moral choices are relative, depending on the situation, but there is also an underlying absolute, a God-given standard of right and wrong.
Authority	Scientific method and findings alone are supreme.	Divine revelation as revealed in the Bible is supreme. Scientific method and findings are important but of secondary importance.

and seeking to discover scientific laws, the scientist is really trying to learn what determines or causes the events and behavior that he observes. Freud expressed this view many years ago when he wrote "There is within you a deeply rooted belief in psychic freedom and choice. . . . This belief is quite unscientific, . . . it must give ground before the claims of a determinism which governs even mental life."[3] The strict determinist position would claim that Paul's conversion experience on the road to Damascus could be explained in terms of the laws of psychology and physiology— if only we knew these laws.[4] Such a view relieves man of both his freedom and responsibility. It makes miracles impossible and leaves no provision for answered prayer or for the influence of God in history.

The Christian recognizes that behavior is molded in large measure by one's childhood experiences and cultural surroundings, but Christians also believe that man has free will and responsibility. Furthermore, although God created an orderly and lawful universe, He is sovereign and can intervene in men's affairs whenever He chooses. Paul's conversion is one such example of divine intervention.

The Christian psychologist recognizes that most behavior can be described within the framework of natural law. Even when men think they are acting freely, their behavior may, in fact, be virtually predetermined by their values and by the culture in which they have been raised. Like other scientists, the Christian psychologist seeks to understand these deterministic laws of behavior through his research and practice. He recognizes, however, that natural law is descriptive, *not* prescriptive, and thus he is compelled to leave room in human experience for both man's choice and God's action.

MAN'S NATURE

Freud and other more modern psychologists have viewed man as basically evil and destructive. A much more common view, however, and one which most psychologists would hold, is that man is basically good. In a famous quotation, Dr. Carl Rogers states this explicitly:

> I do not discover man to be well characterized in his basic nature by such terms as fundamentally hostile, anti-social, destructive, evil.
>
> I do not discover man to be, in his basic nature, completely without a nature, a *tabula rasa* on which *anything* may be written, nor malleable putty which can be shaped into any form.
>
> I do not discover man to be essentially a perfect being, sadly warped and corrupted by society.
>
> In my experiences I have discovered man to have characteristics which seem inherent in his species, and the terms which have at different times seemed to me to be descriptive of these characteristics are such terms as positive, forward-moving, constructive, realistic, trustworthy. [5]

The Christian does not hold such a positive view of man. According to the Bible, man is a being who was divinely created in God's image. But because he chose to rebel, man is now sinful in his nature, alienated from God and from other men, and condemned to be punished. He is also the object of God's redemption and each individual is free either to accept God's redemptive provisions or to remain in sin.

ETHICS

For many years psychologists believed that it was possible to be completely neutral in counseling and research work. Now this is changing and there is increasing recognition that such neutrality is impossible, that all behavior is guided by our personal moral codes and views of what is right or wrong.

In spite of this recognition of the importance of values, the psychologist tends to be a relativist. He holds the view that whether behavior is right or wrong depends on the culture, on the situation, and on the individual. What is right for one individual in one culture or at one period in history may not be right for someone else at another place and time.

The Christian also recognizes that many moral decisions are culture bound and personal. Nevertheless, some laws and behavioral guidelines are laid down by God as absolutes, and revealed in Scripture. Every moral decision must be tested against the moral principles that one finds in the Bible.

The man who is a relativist will view behavior very differently than the man who assumes that there are divinely given absolutes to guide ethical behavior.

AUTHORITY

The psychologist is devoted solely to the scientific method. The only authority for truth is whether an event or act of behavior can be seen by the senses or shown empirically. This belief that the scientific method alone is the key to truth becomes accepted by faith. In some respects, therefore, science can develop into a religion and an object of worship. Its findings become dogma, its methods become ritual, its outstanding researchers become high priests, and its conclusions become authoritative and binding.

The Christian psychologist respects the scientific method and uses it in his research, but he would not agree that the way of science is the *only* path to truth. He realizes that knowledge also comes by God's direct revelation through Scripture. The Bible does not claim to be a scientific textbook and it is silent on most of the matters which concern science. Nevertheless, the Bible is God's Word to man and as such it must be our ultimate authority concerning the matters on which it speaks—directly or indirectly.

ADDITIONAL AREAS OF DISAGREEMENT

In addition to these basic differences in presuppositions, psychology and Christianity also disagree on a number of other issues. One of these is *dualism*—the view that man consists of two parts: body and soul.

DUALISM AND IMMORTALITY

The Bible uses a number of terms to describe the nature of man. In addition to "body" and "soul," the Scriptures speak of the "heart," "spirit," "mind," "flesh," and of an inner and outer man. Many Christians have concluded, therefore, that man consists of separate parts. Some say that he has two parts (body and soul); others identify three parts (body, soul, and spirit).

For purposes of research and analysis, psychologists often divide man into parts and study such aspects as his behavior, neurological functioning, or conscious experience. Few psychologists would accept the view that man has two or three distinct parts, however, and few would make use of terms such as body, soul, or spirit. These terms are poorly defined and far too vague to be studied scientifically. (One dictionary gives twenty-five definitions of soul, thirty-three of spirit, and thirty of body.) [6] Furthermore, psychologists believe that it is possible to understand behavior without using these theological concepts, and for this reason the terms almost never appear in modern texts. Contemporary psychology views man not as a dichotomy or trichotomy. Rather, man is seen as a unity and it is anticipated that further research will eventually demonstrate that his nervous system, muscular movements, glandular secretions, conscious experiences, and unconscious influences all work together as part of a unified whole.

The question of whether or not man has a distinctly separate body, soul, and spirit is of little concern to psychology as a science. *Behavior* is the object of study. Whether or not the individual *behaver* has a body which decays and a soul which lives on after death is beyond empirical study and of little scientific interest. The issue may come up in counseling; however, for the counselee who believes in a

130

soul and afterlife is likely to have values and standards of behavior which reflect this belief in contrast to the opinions of most psychologists who see man as an animal organism that lives for a few years and passes out of existence—except as a memory in the brains of the people who remain.

It is important to note that while all Christians believe in personal immorality (most psychologists apparently do not), all believers do not accept the dualistic or trichotomous view of man. Many would agree with psychologists that man is really a unified whole. G. C. Berkouwer, for example, the respected Dutch theologian, makes a very convincing case for the essential unity of man. The idea of a trichotomy, he points out, originated in Greek philosophy and is not supported in Scripture.

> The Biblical view of man shows him to us in an impressive diversity, but . . . it never loses sight of the unity of the whole man, but rather brings it out and accentuates it.
> No part of man is emphasized as independent of other parts. . . . Thus the various terms and concepts it [the Bible] makes use of give us no exactly expressed or scientifically useful definitions, but rather are related always to the same basic reality of humanness; so that despite the various shifts in terminology, we never receive the impression that we are dealing with an important shift in the portrayal of man. . . .
> It appears clearly, then, that Scripture never pictures man as a dualistic, or pluralistic being, but that in all its varied expressions the whole man comes to the fore, in all his guilt and sin, his need and oppression, his longings and his nostalgia. [7]

THE CONSCIENCE

This term has been defined in various ways, but it is commonly viewed as an inner ability to evaluate whether one's thoughts, acts, or intentions are right or wrong. Apparently the word is used with this connotation in several places in the Bible.

Almost all psychologists agree that an individual's sense

of right and wrong (that is, his conscience) is formed as a result of learning. By observing the behavior and hearing the verbal instructions of parents and other significant people, the young person eventually formulates his personal conceptions of what is morally good and bad. By the time one is an adult his conscience is well-developed, although there may be changes at any time during life. Much of this conscience-development occurs without the individual even being aware that this is happening.

The point of conflict between psychology and Christianity centers around Romans 2:14 and 15. "The Gentiles do not have the Law; but whenever of their own free will they do what the Law commands, they are a law to themselves, even though they do not have the Law. Their consciences show though they do not have the Law. Their conduct shows that what the Law commands is written in their hearts. Their consciences also show that this is true, since their thoughts sometimes accuse them and sometimes defend them" (Today's English Version). This passage is contrasting the behavior of Jews and Gentiles. The former had a written law to guide their behavior; the latter had a law "written in their hearts." When "written in their hearts" is taken to mean "inborn," psychologists are critical of what they assume is a Christian view of conscience. An inborn conscience would contradict all of the psychological evidence which shows that conscience is learned.

The law "written in their hearts" is apparently possessed by adults who are able to act ("do") in some way. Notice that the writer of this passage does not say *how* the conscience was obtained by these adults. Furthermore, none of the other relevant Biblical passages discusses the origin of conscience. Is it possible, therefore, that as men and women mature they develop "in their hearts" ideas about right and wrong which are largely consistent with God's perfect and absolute standards? God, who is the originator of moral values, guides as these are acquired. But because of his sin, man has distorted divine moral values and developed an imperfect conscience. Even when his views of right and wrong are consistent with God's standards, man often acts in ways that go against his conscience. Several research studies demonstrate that a knowledge of right and wrong does not necessarily correspond with one's actions.

The disagreement over the origin of the conscience is reduced, therefore, if we take "written in their hearts" to mean not "inborn," but "acquired under God's guidance as we grow up." Such a view can be consistent with Scripture and in accordance with the findings of psychological research.

WHY ARE PEOPLE RELIGIOUS?

This question has interested men for many years and conflicting answers have led to disagreement between psychologist and Christianity. The English philosopher Bertrand Russell concluded that religion is based on fear—fear of the mysterious, fear of defeat, fear of death. [8] God, Russell suggested, is a human invention who gives men the security of thinking that there is an elder brother who will be near whenever we have troubles or disputes. Freud concluded that religion and the belief in a God has three functions: to reduce our fears of nature and the unknown, to give some meaning to death and other difficult experiences, and to keep society intact. Because he is afraid of what God will do to the person who is antisocial, man acts in ways which are good for society and lead to its preservation. If he was not afraid of God, Freud reasoned, man would do what he pleases when he pleases, and society would soon collapse.* Both Russell and Freud have written that religion and belief in a deity is bad for the individual. Many years ago both expressed hope that as science progressed, religion would

---

*Some have concluded that his, indeed, is what is happening in our society today; we have eliminated God as each man "does his own thing" the civilization is beginning to crumble.

cease to be important or necessary.

As indicated in a previous chapter, many psychologists are becoming more sympathetic to the value of religion. The most prevalent view, however, is still that religion is bad, a carry-over from prescientific times, and a crutch for the emotionally unstable. Christianity is viewed as an opiate or mass tranquilizer which is used by weak, uneducated people, but is no use to the strong, educated, and emotionally stable.

An individual's views concerning the desirability of religion largely result from his personal experience with religion, his understanding of doctrine, and his encounters with religious people. Freud's views arose mostly from his psychiatric practice. Since he only saw religion as experienced by neurotics, he got a distorted view. Furthermore, it is clear that Freud—and most contemporary psychologists—was without understanding of the real nature of Christianity. Since the nonbeliever cannot really comprehend spiritual things (1 Co. 2:14), the secular psychologist sees Christianity as nothing more than a crutch or figment of human imagination.

It cannot be denied that Christianity can be used as a crutch, but there is nothing wrong with leaning on a crutch occasionally. Almost all men do so at times and if used during periods of weakness and later discarded, a crutch can lead to growth and increased strength. When people refuse to grow and continue to lean on their crutches indefinitely, this is unhealthy but it is not the fault of the crutch. Of course, some neurotic people show an unhealthy dependence on their faith but many other Christians mature as persons largely because of their belief in Christ and dependence on Him.

It must not be assumed that Christianity is solely a support for times of distress. It is much more. Belief in Christ gives men a new set of values, a new source of power for living, a meaningful life for the present, and an assurance of eternal life in the future. It also gives men new responsibility and the promise of difficulties. The true follower of Christ does not sit around basking in perpetual happiness. He becomes a servant who can expect to encounter opposition and difficulties. One need only look at the life of Paul to see this. Such an understanding of the truths, joys, and tribulations of Christianity is lacking among most contemporary psychologists. Some can see value in a human-centered form of religion; few can appreciate the biblical basis of Christianity. For this reason disagreements about the value of religion and Christianity will undoubtedly persist.

CONVERSION

Conversion involves a change from one belief to another which is considered to be better. There are many psychological explanations to account for this experience, including the views that conversion is an emotional response to group pressure, a reaction to the frustrations of adolescence, or a finding of new meaning in life by persons who previously were unhappy and dissatisfied. The psychologist works on the presupposition that conversion is a natural event that occurs apart from any known supernatural influences.

The Christian's reaction to such psychological conclusions has been stated by Dr. Vernon Grounds:

> Granted that a person may be born again by a process that includes such conditions as susceptibility to the semi-hypnotic autosuggestion induced by a skillful evangelist in the minds of an emotion-charged crowd, or the struggle of an adolescent to mature, or the unconscious drive of a divided self to achieve unity. Granted that these factors may operate in the conversion experience. The Christian is nevertheless free to argue that the Holy Spirit sovereignly uses just such conditions and just such processes as His means of bringing about a supernatural result. [10]

While conversion to non-Christian religions or to new political beliefs may show some of the characteristics of conversion to Christ, the Christian believes that there is one big difference: Christian conversion involves the transformation of a life by the power of the Holy Spirit. Psychological studies can often explain what takes place when one has a religious experience but psychology cannot account for the change which occurs when an individual commits his life to Christ and experiences the new birth. The psychologist's persuppositions and methods of investigation prevent him from understanding or even studying such a supernatural event.

GUILT

In psychology, guilt can be defined as a realization that one has violated ethical, moral, or religious principles, together with a resulting feeling of regret and lessened personal worth. [11] Guilt is a form of self-blame which all of us feel at times to a greater or lesser extent. Most people accept the existence of guilt, but disagreement over the source, value, and ways of removing guilt has been the cause of considerable conflict between Christianity and psychology.

Most psychologists believe that guilt results either from an action or thought which goes against the dictates of one's conscience, or from a failure to act in accordance with conscience. Guilt results from a human failure to act in accordance with a human moral code. It is generally agreed that guilt is harmful—the cause of many personal problems—and should be overcome.

But how does one overcome guilt? While psychologists have different answers to this question, there are two common views. One is that the conscience should be changed. If one can be convinced that a moral act—like sexual intercourse outside of marriage—is not wrong, then the problem behavior can continue without the accompanying guilt. The other view is to deal with the guilt. By discussing it, trying to understand it, ignoring it, or trying to forget it, the troublesome guilt will hopefully disappear.

136

Within recent years, another psychological view has been gaining preeminence. This view, suggested by Dr. O. H. Mowrer of the University of Illinois, agrees that guilt is at the basis of many of man's problems. Rather than ignoring the guilt or trying to change one's standards, Mowrer believes that the guilty person should confess his "sins" to a significant other person. If a man feels guilty because of his extramarital affairs, for example, he should confess to his wife, ask her forgiveness, and seek to reform his ways. [12]

The Christian reader may have already recognized that these psychological views say nothing about God. This is consistent with psychological presuppositions concerning the sovereignty of man. In contrast, the Christian believes that any consideration of guilt must include some reference to God. Dr. Paul Tournier, the Swiss physician and counselor, has distinguished between two kinds of guilt. [13] False guilt, he suggests, arises when our behavior or thoughts go against man-made standards. When we feel guilty because we have wasted time, made a sarcastic remark, or acted in some other socially undesirable way, we experience false guilt. True guilt, in contrast, is the result of disobedience to God and a failure to act in accordance with His standards. In practice it is usually difficult to separate these two kinds of guilt. Most of our sins against men are also sins against God. The resulting guilt comes because we have acted in ways which are not in accordance with the divine will.

Unlike those psychologists who try to hide or explain away guilt, the Christian believes that guilt, and the sin which caused it, should be faced and confessed. God will forgive our sins and remove our guilt (1 Jn. 1:9). This divine forgiveness is a gift which is in no way dependent on man's actions. Regrettably, because of this, Christians sometimes conclude that one can sin against another man, confess this sin to God, and then forget about it since we are sure of God's forgiveness. But the Bible also instructs us to go to the man whom we have hurt, ask his forgiveness, and then change our behavior so that the sinful act is not repeated (Mt. 5:23-34; Ja. 5:16; Ro. 6:1-2).

Sin and guilt are terms which frequently appear in discussions on abnormal behavior. The disagreements concerning these issues will surely continue so long as Christians believe in a forgiving merciful God, and psychologists do not believe.

MIRACLES

Miracles can be defined as unusual events which have no natural explanations but which are assumed to result from the intervention of some supernatural power. The Bible records numerous miracles and many Christians believe that such supernatural events still occur.

In contrast, most modern psychologists relegate miracles to the superstition of a bygone era. Many years ago, the argument goes, before the age of science, people needed some explanation to account for events which were not easily understood. The simplest explanation was to assume that some unknown supernatural power intervened in men's affairs to bring about a change. With the advance of science we no longer need such speculative arguments. Man is learning that so-called miracles can be explained scientifically. As an example, the psychologist might consider faith healing. We know that much physical illness has a psychological cause. When psychological outlook changes, there is, in turn, an improvement in the physical condition. This is what happens when a sick person encounters a faith healer. Under the healer's persuasive influence the patient may begin to hope that a physical cure is possible. This changed emotional state in turn brings a change in physical functioning and an improvement in the believer's condition. The healing is not miraculous. It can be explained scientifically. The psychologist believes that all miracles will eventually be explained in a similar manner.

The psychologist works on the assumption that there is no God. If this is so, there can be no supernatural influences in human events and miracles are impossible. To be consistent with his presuppositions, the psychologist explains away miracles and to do so he appeals to science.

The Christian recognizes that some of the miracles recorded in the Bible appear to be explainable by science but there are many others which cannot be explained. Even if logical scientific explanations for most miracles do appear in the future, this does not eliminate God. Instead it shows how God works. What was once a mystery becomes understood as God reveals some of His workings to men.

Christianity assumes that all events occur within the sphere of God's providential supervision and control (Col. 1:17; Heb. 1:3). Occasionally God speeds up His work and the resulting event is called a miracle. When a man is sick, for example, God usually heals through such techniques as the influence of medicines and work of the white corpuscles. Occasionally, however, God bypasses this process and cures immediately in some unexplained manner. The Christian calls this a miracle. The psychologist does not believe it can happen.

DEMON POSSESSION

Like miracles, demon possession is only of historical interest to psychology. When primitive man could not understand the reasons for abnormal behavior, he guessed that some evil spirit must have control of the person. "Treatment" consisted of torture in order to drive out the spirit.

There can be no doubt that many of the historical beliefs about demons were largely the result of creative imaginations and even many modern church leaders have chosen to "write off" demonology as an outdated superstition. There are other Christians, however, who believe that demons did and still do exist. Jesus, the one who claimed to be God and "the truth," believed in demons and ordered them to come out of individuals. Paul warned that Christians must wrestle against these spiritually wicked forces (Eph. 6:12). While demon possession is probably not a very adequate explanation for abnormal behavior, there is clear Biblical evidence that evil forces exist even today to influence men's behavior. Once again psychology's naturalistic presuppositions forbid recognition of such supernatural powers.

THE PROBLEM OF INTEGRATION

How does the Christian who is a student of psychology integrate the opposing presuppositions and conclusions of psychology and Christianity? This is a difficult task and some Christian psychologists believe that such integration is impossible. When the subject matter of psychology is far removed from Christianity, it is relatively easy to be double-minded. The Christian psychologist can worship God when in his church or at home; he can run rats through mazes, collect survey data, administer psychological tests, or perform learning experiments in his laboratory; and the two areas of interest need never conflict. Much of the subject matter of psychology has no conflict with Christianity. It can be accepted by both psychologists and church leaders because the conflicting presuppositions are kept in the background. Often the psychological conclusions do not appear to contradict the truths of Scripture and may not even be discussed in the Bible.

But the opposing presuppositions still exist and they cannot always be ignored by the Christian psychologist. Likewise the findings of psychology sometimes *do* contradict the conclusions of theology and the statements of the Bible. At such times there are four possible ways in which the conflicts can be handled. [14]

First is to conclude that the terms and concepts of psychology and Christianity are really interchangeable. Since the two fields are assumed to be dealing with the same issues but from two different perspectives, there is no real conflict. This chapter has surely shown that such a view is over-simplified and untenable. Psychology and Christianity employ different languages and presuppositions and have arrived at many conflicting conclusions.

A second view sees psychology as asking questions and theology providing answers. While this does occur to some extent, a rigid adherence to such a view would lead to continued conflict and confusion. The psychologist, with his presuppositions and methods, would be likely to ask questions which the theologian, with his presuppositions and methods, could not answer and would have no interest in answering. Psychology and theology each ask and seek to answer many questions which are of no concern to the other discipline.

A third view is much more tenable. It assumes that there is a dominance-subservience relationship in which psychology holds the upper hand. This is undoubtedly the view held by many church leaders and almost all psychologists. When there is disagreement between psychology and theology, the findings of scientific psychology—in spite of their transient and often conflicting nature—are assumed to be true.

The fourth view also assumes a dominance-subservience relationship but in this case theology has the preeminence. When the words of the Bible and the findings of psychology are in contradiction and there does not appear to be any hope of integration, the theological position is assumed to be correct.

The Christian psychologist is likely to accept a view which is a variation of this fourth position. Psychologist Paul Meehl states this clearly:

> He takes it for granted that revelation cannot genuinely *contradict* any truths about man or the world which are discoverable by other means (including science). If such appears to have happened, he must operate on the assumption that this is only an appearance. That being presupposed, he then

seeks to resolve the contradiction . . . If a resolution cannot be effected, the problem is put on the shelf as a mystery, not solvable by the lights of nature or of grace but only in light of glory. [15]

When there is disagreement, the fault may lie with inaccurate or incomplete scientific knowledge, or with incorrect biblical interpretation. If one has to make a decision, the revelation of God must take precedence over the conclusions of science. Since the Bible is not a scientific textbook, however, it is silent concerning many of the issues which concern psychologists. Likewise, scientific psychology ignores many of the issues of theology. The major areas of contact and conflict between psychology and Christianity are those that have been briefly considered in this chapter. These are the issues where psychology and Christianity meet—and sometimes lock horns.

SUMMARY

Psychology and Christianity are both concerned, among other things, with the study of behavior. To a large extent the psychologist conducts his research and reaches his conclusions about behavior, the theologian does the same, and the student of each discipline works at problems which are of no concern to the other field. There are many issues, however, in which the findings of psychology and theology are in sharp contrast. There are disagreements, for instance, over the question of whether man is a one-part or two-part creature, the origin and influence of conscience, the significance of religious faith, the nature of conversion, the importance of guilt, the credibility of miracles, and the existence of demons.

These disagreements partially result from differences in language. Psychology and theology each use terms which have no precise meaning in the other field. The main basis for disagreement, however, lies in the conflicting presuppositions. The Christian and the psychologist have different views of the world in which we live, the extent to which behavior is determined by the laws of nature, the nature of man, the basis for ethical decisions, and the source of all truth. Because of these differing assumptions there are differences in many of the conclusions reached by psychology and Christianity.

The best way to resolve such differences is to collect more information. When genuine contradictions still exist, it is common to assume either that psychology is always right, or that Christianity is always preeminent. The Christian psychologist assumes that divine revelation and the true facts of science cannot genuinely contradict. When a contradiction is apparent, he must continue to seek for facts or put the issue aside while he waits for further evidence.

EPILOGUE

During my days as a graduate student, I had a professor who had the habit of repeatedly asking a very disturbing question. Whenever a student would write a paper or we would study a research report, this professor would invariably lean back in his chair and quietly ask, "So what?" Having read through this book and perhaps the ones that preceeded it, the thoughtful reader, like my former professor, might be wise to ask the same question. "So what?" Perhaps the preceeding pages have seemed interesting or dull, clearly written or incomprehensible, applicable or completely irrelevant, but so what? Can this psychological knowledge have any practical value and if so, where do we go from here?

It is inevitable, I suppose, that some readers will put the books of this series back on the shelf, having concluded that the author and psychology in general, say little of value for the church leader. I would hope, however, that for many more there will be a recognition that the insights and findings of psychology can and do have real relevance to many aspects of the Lord's work. For people who feel this way, the following suggestions should be helpful.

First, try now to apply what has been presented. If a knowledge of psychology does increase self-understanding, an understanding of others and our skillfulness in working with people—as I believe it does—then we should actively seek to improve in these areas, making use of the information that has been presented.

Second, evaluate yourself and your work. We need to be continually looking at our work, trying to overcome weaknesses, and seeking for better ways of doing things. Hopefully the preceeding pages have alerted us to ways in which we might change and improve our effectiveness.

Third, keep learning. We need to keep reading as much as time permits and for this reason at the end of the book there is a list of books for additional study. As you read these, keep asking, "So what? How can this help me to do a, better job?"

Finally, remember to keep psychology in its proper perspective. I have attempted to show that "psychology is a valuable tool which church leaders, seeking the guidance of the Holy Spirit, can use in their Christian service." But psychology must never become *the* work of the church. If kept in perspective—as a supplement to the work of Christ's church—psychology can have real value for all Christians, and especially for those who are church leaders. Hopefully, the four volumes of the *Psychology for Church Leaders* series will contribute to this end.

NOTES

Chapter 1

1. Theories of learning have been summarized by E. R. Hilgard and G. H. Bower, *Theories of Learning*; and W. F. Hill, *Learning: A Survey of Psychological Interpretations*.
2. G. Razran, "Partial Reinforcement of Salivary CR's in Adult Human Subjects," *Psychological Reports* 1 (1955): 409-16.
3. J. B. Watson and R. Rayner, "Conditioned Emotional Reactions," *Journal of Experimental Psychology* 3 (1920): 1-14.
4. H. E. Jones and M. C. Jones, "Learning to Fear," in *Basic Contributions to Psychology: Readings*, ed. R. L. Wrenn, pp. 153-56.
5. G. D. Wright, "A Further Note on Ranking the Important Psychologists," *American Psychologist* 25 (1970): 650-51.
6. The present discussion is adapted from an earlier book by the author, *Search for Reality: Psychology and the Christian*, pp. 172-76.
7. B. F. Skinner, *The Technology of Teaching*.
8. R. Ulrich, et. al., eds. *Control of Human Behavior;* C. Neuringer and J. L. Michael, *Behavior Modification in Clinical Psychology;* F. H. Kanfer and J. S. Phillips, *Learning Foundations of Behavior Therapy;* A. Lazarus, *Behavior Therapy and Beyond;* and M. Karlins and L. M. Andrews, *Man Controlled*.
9. The ethics of such behavior manipulation have been discussed at length elsewhere (see the articles by Moberg and by Collins in the *Journal of the American Affiliation*, March, 1970). In a sense education is an attempt to manipulate the behavior of others. Like guns and drugs, however, the manipulation of behavior can be both for man's good and for man's harm. We must work for the former and try to prevent the latter.
10. This discussion is not meant to imply that all churches are dead. Many are exciting places that meet a real spiritual, emotional, and social need in the lives of members. See, for example, D. Mains, *Full Circle*.
11. B. F. Skinner, *Walden Two*.
12. R. L. Solomon, "Punishment," *American Psychologist* 19 (1964): 239-53.
13. R. M. Church, "The Varied Effects of Punishment on Behavior," *Psychological Review* 70 (1963): 369-402; and D. M. Baer, "Let's Take Another Look at Punishment," *Psychology Today* 5 (Oct. 1971): 32-37, 111.
14. H. C. Ellis, *The Transfer of Learning*; and J. Deese and S. H. Hulse, *The Psychology of Learning*.
15. H. J. Klausmeier and R. E. Ripple, *Learning and Human Abilities*.
16. P. M. Fitts, "Factors in Complex Learning," in *Training Research and Education*, R. Glass, ed.
17. Klausmeier and Ripple.
18. J. Kagan and E. Havemann, *Psychology: An Introduction*.
19. J. Kagan, *Personality Development*.
20. S. L. Pressey, "A Simple Apparatus Which Gives Tests and Scores and Teaches," *School and Society* 23 (1926): 373-76.
21. B. F. Skinner, "The Science of Learning and the Art of Teaching," *Harvard Educational Review* 24 (1954): 86-97.
22. B. F. Skinner, "Teaching Machines," *Science* 128 (1958): 969-77.

23. W. I. Smith and J. W. Moore, eds., *Programmed Learning*; and J. W. Leib, "Teaching Machines and Programmed Instruction: Areas of Application," *Psychological Bulletin* 67 (1967): 12-26.
24. B. F. Skinner, *The Technology of Teaching.*
25. W. M. Gilbert and T. N. Ewing, "Programmed Versus Face-to-Face Counseling," *Journal of Consulting Psychology* 18 (1971): 413-21.
26. T. A. Wilkinson and G. R. Collins, "Programmed Religious Instruction," Unpublished manuscript, 1971.
27. R. H. Roth, "Student Reactions to Programmed Learning," *Phi Delta Kappan* (Mar. 1963): 278-81; and L. J. Kazmier, "Repeated Exposure to Programmed Instruction and Student Attitude," *Psychological Reports* 19 (1966): 985-86.
28. D. M. Brethower, *Programmed Instruction.*
29. See, for example, L. S. Cermak, *Human Memory and Learning.*
30. W. Penfield, *The Excitable Cortex in Conscious Man.*
31. L. M. Harden, "Effect of Emotional Reactions Upon Retention," *Journal of General Psychology* 3 (1930): 197-221.
32. R. F. Mager, *Preparing Instructional Objectives*; and B. F. Skinner, *The Technology of Teaching.*

Chapter 2

1. R. Wolff, *The Meaning of Loneliness.*
2. W. B. Webb, *Sleep: An Experimental Approach.*
3. R. F. Thompson, *Foundations of Physiological Psychology.*
4. N. L. Munn, L. D. Fernald, Jr., and P. S. Fernald, *Introduction to Psychology.*
5. J. D. Matarazzo, "The Interview," in *Handbook of Clinical Psychology*, ed. B. B. Wolman.
6. D. Combs and A. W. Snygg, *Individual Behavior.*
7. T. Trabasso, "Pay Attention," *Psychology Today* 2 (Oct. 1968): 30-36.
8. I have discussed some of the more common emotions, like anger anxiety, loneliness, discouragement, etc., in *A Psychologist Looks at Life.*
9. W. E. Blatz, "The Cardiac, Respiratory and Electrical Phenomena Involved in the Emotion of Fear," *Journal of Experimental Psychology* 8 (1925): 109-32.
10. M. D. Vernon, *Human Motivation*; and R. S. Lazarus, J. R. Averill and E. M. Opton, Jr., "Toward a Cognitive Theory of Emotion," in *Feelings and Emotions*, ed. M. B. Arnold.
11. M. C. Tenney, *New Testament Survey.*
12. E. Trueblood, *The Humor of Christ.*
13. A. H. Maslow, *Motivation and Personality*, p. 46.
14. S. Z. Klausner, ed., *Why Man Takes Chances.*
15. D. Fiske and S. D. Maddi, *Functions of Varied Experience*; and G. R. Collins, "Optimal Level of Stimulation," Unpublished doctoral dissertation, 1963.
16. W. H. Bexton, W. Heron, and T. H. Scott, "Effects of Decreased Variation in the Sensory Environment," *Canadian Journal of Psychology* 8 (1954): 70-76.
17. see *Man in Transition*, p. 96.
18. A. H. Strong, *Systematic Theology*, p. 339.

Chapter 3

1. L. E. Tyler, *The Psychology of Individual Differences.*
2. L. M. Terman and M. A. Merrill, *Stanford-Binet Intelligence Scale.*
3. V. Packard, *The Status Seekers.*

4. R. A. Heber, "Modifications in the Manual of Terminology and Classification in Mental Retardation," *American Journal of Mental Deficiency* 65 (1961): 499-500.
5. V. E. Anderson, "Chromosomes and Human Behavior," *Journal of the American Scientific Affiliation* 21 (June 1969): 48-49.
6. M. S. Caldwell, "Pastoral Care of Parents of Mentally Retarded Children," in W. E. Oates and 'A. D. Lester, *Pastoral Care in Crucial Human Situations.*
7. R. Perske, "The Pastoral Care and Counseling of Families of the Mentally Retarded," *Pastoral Psychology* 19 (Nov. 1968): 21-28; and S. D. Peterson, "The Pastoral Care of Parents of Mentally Retarded Persons," *Pastoral Psychology* 13 (Sept. 1962): 37-44.
8. M. S. Caldwell, "Pastoral Care of Parents of Mentally Retarded Children."
9. H. W. Stubblefield, "On Being a Pastor to the Mentally Retarded," *Journal of Pastoral Care* 24 (June 1970): 98-108.
10. American Psychological Association, "Psychology and Mental Retardation," *American Psychologist* 25 (1970): 267-68.
11. The books by H. R. Hahn and W. R. Raasch, *Helping the Retarded to Know God,* and by E. Towns and R. Groff, *Successful Ministry to the Retarded,* discuss some of these techniques.
12. E. S. Golden, "Pastoral Counseling and Guidance with the Mental Retardate," *Pastoral Psychology* 13 (Sept. 1962): 31-36.
13. L. M. Terman, "The Discovery and Encouragement of Exceptional Talent," *American Psychologist* 9 (June 1954): 221-30; and E. W. Telford and J. M. Sawrey, *The Exceptional Individual.*
14. L. M. Bachtold and E. E. Werner, "Personality Profiles of Gifted Women: Psychologists," *American Psychologist* 25 (Mar. 1970): 234-43.
15. J. C. Gowan, "The Underachieving Gifted Child—A Problem for Everyone," *Exceptional Children* 21 (Apr. 1955): 247-71.
16. E. H. Grothberg, "Adjustment Problems of the Gifted," in *Psychology and Education of the Gifted,* ed. W. B. Barbe.
17. W. B. Barbe and E. C. Frierson, "Teaching the Gifted: A New Frame of Reference," in Barbe.
18. A. Anastasi, *Differential Psychology.*
19. N. L. Munn, L. D. Fernald, Jr., and P. S. Fernald, *Introduction to Psychology,* p. 667.
20. E. Trueblood, *The Incendiary Fellowship.*
21. E. K. Strong, "Permanence of Interest Scores over 22 Years," *Journal of Applied Psychology* 35 (1951): 89-91; and "Changes of Interest with Age," in R. G. Kuhlen and G. G. Thompson, *Psychological Studies of Human Development.*
22. Strong, "Satisfactions and Interests," *American Psychologist* 13 (1958): 449-56.
23. H. O. J. Brown, *The Protest of a Troubled Protestant.*
24. J. L. Holland, *The Psychology of Vocational Choice.*

Chapter 4

1. V. Packard, *The Status Seekers.*
2. D. O. Moberg, *The Church as a Social Institution.*
3. C. Reid, *Groups Alive—Church Alive.*
4. R. A. Edgar, "The Listening Structured Group," *Pastoral Psychology* 15 (June 1964): 7-13.

5. C. Reid, *Groups Alive—Church Alive.*
6. H. C. Lindgren, *An Introduction to Social Psychology.*
7. E. L. Hartley and R. L. Hartley, *Fundamentals of Social Psychology.*
8. See, for example, H. Thielicke, *The Trouble with the Church.*
9. S. B. Babbage, *The Vacuum of Unbelief,* p. 128.
10. S. E. Asch, *Social Psychology.*
11. D. Krech, R. S. Crutchfield, and E. L. Ballachey, *Individual in Society.*
12. *Man in Transition,* p. 173.
13. P. F. Secord and C. W. Backman, *Social Psychology.*
14. Secord and Backman; and G. E. Simpson and J. M. Yinger, *Racial and Cultural Minorities.*
15. C. Y. Glock and R. Stark, *Christian Beliefs and Anti-Semitism;* and R. Stark, et. al., "Sounds of Silence," *Psychology Today* 3 (Apr. 1970): 38-41, 60-61.
16. R. C. L. Brannon, "Gimme that Old Time Racism," *Psychology Today* 3 (Apr. 1970): 42-44.
17. R. L. Rosnow, "Poultry and Prejudice," *Psychology Today* 5 (Mar. 1972): 53-56.
18. R. B. Zuck, and G. A. Getz, *Christian Youth.*
19. I. L. Janis, et. al., *Personality and Persuasibility.*
20. M. Rokeach, "Persuasion that Persists," *Psychology Today* 5 (Sept. 1971): 68.
21. W. J. McGuire, "A Vaccine for Brainwash," *Psychology Today* 3 (1970): 36-39, 63-64.
22. McGuire and McGuire, "Inducing Resistance to Persuasion," in L. Berkowitz, *Advances in Experimental Social Psychology,* vol. 1; and Secord and Backman; and D. Papageorges, "Warning and Persuasion," *Psychological Bulletin* 70 (1968): 271-82.
23. Hartley and Hartley.
24. Lindgren.
25. R. F. Bales, "Task Roles and Social Roles in Problem Solving Groups," in E. E. Maccobby, et. al., *Readings in Social Psychology.*
26. D. Cartwright, and A. Zander, eds., *Group Dynamics.*
27. Lindgren.
28. Lindgren.
29. Lindgren.
30. K. Lewin, R. Lippitt, and R. K. White, "Patterns of Aggressive Behavior in Experimentally Created Social Climates," *Journal of Social Psychology* 10 (1939): 271-99; Lippitt and White, "An Experimental Study of Leadership and Group Life," in Maccoby; and White and Lippitt, "Leader Behavior and Member Reaction in Three Social Climates," in Cartwright and Zander.

Chapter 5

1. J. Havens, *Psychology and Religion,* p. 1.
2. E. Fromm, *Man for Himself.*
3. S. Freud, *New Introductory Lectures on Psychoanalysis.*
4. P. Meehl, et. al., *What, Then, Is Man?*
5. C. R. Rogers, "The Nature of Man," *The Nature of Man in Theological and Psychological Perspective,* ed. S. Doninger, p. 91.
6. Meehl, *What, Then, Is Man?*
7. G. C. Berkouwer, *Man: The Image of God,* pp. 200-203.
8. B. Russell, *Why I Am Not a Christian.*
9. S. Freud, *The Future of an Illusion.*

10. V. Grounds, "Psychiatry and Christianity: Conversion," *His* 24 (Nov. 1963): 29.
11. H. B. English, and A. C. English, *A Comprehensive Dictionary of Psychological and Psychoanalytical Terms.*
12. O. H. Mowrer, *The Crisis in Psychiatry and Religion.*
13. P. Tournier, *Guilt and Grace.*
14. Grounds, "Psychiatry and Christianity: Tensions," *His* 23 (Jan. 1963): 14-16, 21-24.
15. Meehl, p. 181.

SUGGESTIONS FOR FURTHER READING

Chapter 1

The psychology of learning is a highly technical and complex subject. In writing this chapter I have been tempted at times to define and use terms like *generalization, discrimination, extinction, inhibition,* or *schedules of reinforcement.* This temptation was resisted because of a desire to make this chapter practical and because learning terms such as these are defined and discussed in almost every introductory psychology textbook. *Introduction to Psychology* by Munn, Fernald and Fernald, is an example.

For the advanced student who wants a complete summary of what psychologists know about learning, see Deese and Hulse's *The Psychology of Learning*, Hall's book by the same title, or Travers' *Essentials of Learning.* Shorter and simpler introductions have been written by Jones, *Learning**, Borger and Seaborns, *The Psychology of Learning**, Mednick, *Learning**, Keller, *Learning: Reinforcement Theory**. Books by Kanfer and Phillips, *Learning Foundations of Behavior Therapy*, by Ulrich, et. al., *Control of Human Behavior**, and by Karlins and Andrews, *Man Controlled*, are technical but fascinating accounts of how learning principles can be used to change people's behavior.

There are a number of good books dealing with Christian education in the local church. Among these are Richards' *Creative Bible Teaching*, and Gangel's *Understanding Teaching.*

Chapter 2

In addition to general psychology textbooks, Dember's *Psychology of Perception* is an excellent technical introduction to the field. Less technical are Leibowitz' *Visual Perception** and Vernon's *The Psychology of Perception**, but none of these books has any direct linkage of perception with the church.

Feelings and Emotions by Arnold and Izard's *The Face of Emotion* are recent discussions of emotion but both are highly technical. Much more readable and directly applicable to emotion is the church is Greenway's *This Emotionalism.*

There are a number of books on motivation, although here again most are technical and of little relevance to the church leader. Bolles' *Theory of Motivation* and Vernon's *Human Motivation** are among the better technical works. More limited to specific topics are Brown's *Isolation**, Singer's *Daydreaming** and Maslow's *Motivation and Personality.**

*Available in paperback editions.

The lack of books dealing with perception, emotion, and motivation in the church reflects the extent to which these three subfields have been ignored by pastoral psychologists.

Chapter 3

The two most basic works in the area of individual differences are those written by Anastasi, *Differential Psychology: Individual and Group Differences in Behavior* and by Tyler, *The Psychology of Human Differences*. Personality differences are discussed in *The Study of Personality* by Norbeck, Price-Williams and McCord, while a little book by Kelly, *Assessment of Human Characteristics** tells how individual differences are measured. These books are all somewhat technical, however, and they make no reference to individual differences in the church.

More relevant to the church leader are books which deal with the intellectually gifted and retarded. Kemp's *The Church, The Gifted and The Retarded Child* is somewhat outdated but still of value. More recent are Hahn and Raasch, *Helping the Retarded to Know God** and Towns and Groff, *Successful Ministry to the Retarded.** A survey of the literature will reveal that there are really very few books dealing with individual differences and the church.

Chapter 4

Moberg's *The Church as a Social Institution* is a classic textbook, written by a very competent sociologist who is also an evangelical. Theologically conservative writers write most of the chapters in a book edited by Larson, *Groups That Work**, and the reader might also want to look at Reid's *Groups Alive—Church Above* and Olmstead's *The Small Group.** The Olmstead book discusses groups in general but makes no reference to the church.

Two little paperback books discuss how people can get along within the church. The author's book on interpersonal relations, *Living in Peace** and Bell's *How to Get Along with People in the Church** are both written for the layman.

The following books discuss some of the other topics that have been considered in this chapter. Allport's *The Nature of Prejudice** is technical but well worth wading through. Brown's *Techniques of Persuasion** is a general introduction, while *Persuasion: How Opinions and Attitudes are Changed** by Karlins and Abelson gives a number of very practical suggestions. McLaughlin's *Communication for the Church* is very helpful, although somewhat outdated, while Gangel's *Leadership for Church Education* is recent and practical. Both McLaughlin and Gangel are competent evangelicals.

Chapter 5

A general overview of the issues confronting science and Christianity is presented in MacKay's *Christianity in a Mechanistic Universe** and Jeeves' *The Scientific Enterprise and Christian Faith*. For a detailed and scholarly discussion of the relationships between psychology and theology, the reader would benefit from study of the Lutheran symposium *What, Then, Is Man?* by Meehl. More popular treatments of the same topic are contained in a series of articles* which Vernon Grounds wrote for *His* magazine* (beginning in January, 1963), in the chapter on psychology

---

*Available in paperback editions.

by Stanley E. Lindquist in *The Encounter Between Christianity and Science* edited by Bube, and in the author's *Search for Reality: Psychology and the Christian.**

Some of the specific issues discussed in this chapter are more fully considered in Lewis' *Miracles**; Mowrer's *The Crisis in Psychiatry and Religion**; Ferm's *The Psychology of Christian Conversion*; Tournier's *Guilt and Grace*; Knight's *Conscience and Guilt*; Belgum's *Guilt: Where Religion and Psychology Meet**; Outler's *Psychiatry and the Christian Message*: Roberts' *Psychotherapy and a Christian View of Man**, Strunk's *Readings in the Psychology of Religion*, and Thouless' *An Introduction to the Psychology of Religion**.

The literature on this subject is enormous, and each of the sources listed above makes reference to other excellent publications.

*Available in paperback editions.

BIBLIOGRAPHY

Allport, G. W. *The Nature of Prejudice.* Garden City: Doubleday, Anchor Books, 1954.

American Psychological Association. "Psychology and Mental Retardation." *American Psychologist* 25 (Mar. 1970): 267-68.

Anastasi, A. *Differential Psychology: Individual and Group Differences in Behavior.* 3d ed. New York: Macmillan, 1958.

Anderson, V. E. "Chromosomes and Human Behavior." *Journal of the American Scientific Affiliation* 21 (June 1969): 48-49.

Arnold, M., ed. *Feelings and Emotions: The Loyloa Symposium.* New York: Academic Press, 1970.

Asch, S. E. *Social Psychology.* Englewood Cliffs: Prentice-Hall, 1952.

Babbage, S. B. *The Vacuum of Unbelief.* Grand Rapids: Zondervan, 1969.

Bachtold, L. M. and Werner, E. E. "Personality Profiles of Gifted Women: Psychologists." *American Psychologist* 25 (Mar. 1970): 234-43.

Baer, D. M. "Let's Take Another Look at Punishment." *Psychology Today* 5 (Oct. 1971): 32-37, 111.

Bales, R. F. "Task Roles and Social Roles in Problem-solving Groups." *Readings in Social Psychology.* 3d ed. Edited by E. E. Maccoby, T. M. Newcomb, and E. L. Hartley. New York: Holt, Rinehart and Winston, 1958. 437-46.

Barbe, W. B. and Frierson, E. C. "Teaching the Gifted—a New Frame of Reference." *Psychology and Education of the Gifted: Selected Readings.* Edited by W. B. Barbe. New York: Appleton-Century-Crofts, 1965, 321-24.

Belgum, D. *Guilt: Where Religion and Psychology Meet.* Minneapolis: Augsburg, 1970.

Bell, A. Donald. *How to Get Along With People in the Church.* Grand Rapids: Zondervan, 1960.

Bennis, W. G. and Shepard, H. "A Theory of Group Development." *Human Relations* 9 (1956): 415-37.

Berkouwer, G. C. *Man: The Image of God.* Grand Rapids: Eerdmans, 1962.

Bexton, W. H., Heron, W. and Scott, T. H. "Effects of Decreased Variation in the Sensory Environment." *Canadian Journal of Psychology* 8 (1954): 70-76.

Blatz, W. E. "The Cardiac, Respiratory, and Electrical Phenomena Involved in the Emotion of Fear." *Journal of Experimental Psychology* 8 (1925): 109-32.

Bolles, R. C. *Theory of Motivation.* New York: Harper and Row, 1967.

Borger, R. and Seaborne, A. E. M. *The Psychology of Learning.* Baltimore: Penguin, 1966.

Brannon, R. C. L. "Gimme That Old-time Racism." *Psychology Today* 3 (Apr. 1970): 42-44.

Brethower, D. M. *Programmed Instruction: A Manual of Programming Techniques.* Chicago: Educational Methods, 1963.

Brown, C. A. *Isolation: Clinical and Experimental Approaches.* New York: Random House, 1965.

Brown, H. O. J. *The Protest of a Troubled Protestant.* Grand Rapids: Zondervan, 1969.

Brown, J. A. C. *Techniques of Persuasion: From Propaganda to Brainwashing.* Baltimore: Penguin Books, 1963.

Bube, R. H., ed. *The Encounter Between Christianity and Science.* Grand Rapids: Eerdmans, 1968.

Caldwell, M. S. "Pastoral Care of Parents of Mentally Retarded Children." *Pastoral Care in Crucial Human Situations.* Edited by W. E. Oates and A. D. Lester. Valley Forge: Judson Press, 1969, 44-61.

Cartwright, D. and Zander, A., eds. *Group Dynamics.* Evanston: Row, Peterson, 1953.

Cermak, L. S. *Human Memory and Learning.* New York: Ronald, 1972.

Church, R. M. "The Varied Effects of Punishment on Behavior." *Psychological Review 70* (1963): 369-402.

Cofer, C. N. *Motivation and Emotion.* Glenview: Scott, Foresman, 1971.

Collins, G. R. *Living in Peace: The Psychology of Interpersonal Relations.* Wheaton: Key, 1970.

———. "The Manipulation of Human Behavior: A Psychologist's Perspective." *Journal of the American Scientific Affiliation* 22 (Mar. 1970): 8-13.

———. "Optimal Level of Stimulation." Unpublished doctoral dissertation. Purdue University, 1963.

———. *A Psychologist Looks at Life.* Wheaton: Key, 1971.

———. *Search for Reality: Psychology and the Christian.* Wheaton: Key, 1969.

Combs, A. W. and Snygg, D. *Individual Behavior: A Perceptual Approach to Behavior.* Rev. ed. New York: Harper, 1959.

Deese, J. and Hulse, S. H. *The Psychology of Learning.* 3d. ed. New York: McGraw-Hill, 1967.

Dember, W. N. *The Psychology of Perception.* New York: Henry Holt and Company, 1960.

Doninger, S., ed. *The Nature of Man in Theological and Psychological Perspective.* New York: Harper, 1962.

Edgar, R. A. "The Listening Structured Group." *Pastoral Psychology* 15 (June, 1964): 7-13.

Ellis, H. C. *The Transfer of Learning.* New York: Macmillan, 1965.

English, H. B. and English, Ava C. *A Comprehensive Dictionary of Psychological and Psychoanalytical Terms.* New York: Longmans, Green, 1958.

Ferm, R. O. *The Psychology of Christian Conversion.* Westwood: Revell, 1959.

Fiske, D. and Maddi, S. R. *Functions of Varied Experience.* Homewood: Dorsey Press, 1961.

Fitts, P. M. "Factors in Complex Learning." *Training Research and Education.* Edited by R. Glaser. New York: Wiley, 1965.

Frued, S. *The Future of an Illusion.* Garden City. *New Introductory Lectures on Psycho-analysis.* New York: Norton, 1933.

Fromm, E. *Man for Himself.* New York: Rinehart & Company, Inc., 1947.

Gangel, K. O. *Leadership for Church Education.* Chicago: Moody, 1970.

Gilbert, W. M. and Ewing, T. N. "Programmed Versus Face-to-Face Counseling." *Journal of Consulting Psychology* 18 (1971): 413-21.

Glock, C. Y. and Stark, R. *Christian Beliefs and Anti-semitism.* New York: Harper & Row, 1966.

Golden, E. S. "Pastoral Counseling and Guidance with the Mental Retardate." *Pastoral Psychology* 13 (Sept. 1962): 31-36.

Gowan, J. C. "The Underachieving Gifted Child—A Problem for Everyone." *Exceptional Children.* 21 (Apr. 1955): 247-71.

Greenway, W. H. *This Emotionalism.* London: Victory Press, 1954.

Grothberg, E. H. "Adjustment Problems of the Gifted." *Psychology and Education of the Gifted: Selected Readings.* Edited by W. B. Barbe. New York: Appleton-Century-Crofts, 1965.

Grounds, V. "Psychiatry and Christianity: Conversion." *His* 24 (Nov. 1963): 26-31, 34.

———. "Psychiatry and Christianity: Tensions." *His* 23 (Jan. 1963): 14-16, 21-24.

Hahn, H. R. and Raasch, W. R. *Helping the Retarded to Know God.* St. Louis: Concordia, 1969.

Hall, J. F. *The Psychology of Learning.* Philadelphia: Lippincott, 1966.

Harden, L. M. "Effect of Emotional Reactions Upon Retention." *Journal of General Psychology* 3 (1930): 197-221.

Hartley, E. L. and Hartley, R. E. *Fundamentals of Social Psychology.* New York: Alfred A. Knopf, 1952.

Havens, J., ed. *Psychology and Religion: A Contemporary Dialogue.* Princeton: Van Nostrand, 1968.

Heber, R. A. "Modifications in the Manual on Terminology and Classification in Mental Retardation." *American Journal of Mental Deficiency* 65 (1961): 499-500.

Hill, Winfred F. *Learning: A Survey of Psychological Interpretations.* San Francisco: Chandler, 1963.

Hilgard, E. R. and Bower, G. H. *Theories of Learning.* 3d. ed. New York: Appleton-Century-Crofts, 1966.

Holland, J. L. *The Psychology of Vocational Choice.* Waltham: Blaisdell, 1966.

Izard, C. E. *The Face of Emotion.* New York: Appleton-Century-Crofts, 1971.

Janis, I. L., et. al. *Personality and Persuasibility.* New Haven: Yale University Press, 1959.

———. "Groupthink." *Psychology Today* 5 (Nov. 1971): 43-46, 74-76.

———. Mahl, G. F., Kagan, J. and Holt, R. R. *Personality: Dynamics, Development and Assessment.* New York: Harcourt, Brace & World, 1969.

Jeeves, M. A. *The Scientific Enterprise and Christian Faith.* Downers Grove: Inter-Varsity, 1969.

Jones, H. E. and Jones, M. C. "Learning to Fear." *Basic Contributions to Psychology: Readings.* Edited by R. L. Wrenn. Belmont: Wadsworth, 1966, 153-156.

Jones, J. C. *Learning.* New York: Harcourt, Brace, & World, 1967.

Kagan, J. *Personality Development.* New York: Harcourt, Brace, Jovanovich, 1971.

——— and Havemann, E. *Psychology: An Introduction.* 2d ed. New York: Harcourt, Brace, Jovanovich, 1971.

Kanfer, F. H. and Phillips, J. S. *Learning Foundations of Behavior Therapy.* New York: Wiley, 1970.

Karlins, M. and Abelson, H. I. *Persuasion: How Opinions and Attitudes are Changed.* New York: Springer, 1970.

– – – and Andrews, L. M. *Man Controlled: Readings in the Psychology of Behavior Control*. Riverside: The Free Press, 1971.

Kazmier, L. J. "Repeated Exposure to Programmed Instruction and Student Attitude." *Psychological Reports* 19 (1966): 985-86.

Keller, F. S. *Learning: Reinforcement Theory*. Rev. ed. New York: Random, 1969.

Kelly, E. L. *Assessment of Human Characteristics*. Belmont: Brooks, Cole, 1967.

Kemp, C. F. *The Church: The Gifted and the Retarded Child*. St. Louis: Bethany, 1957.

Keniston, K. *Young Radicals: Notes on Committed Youth*. New York: Harcourt, Brace & World, 1968.

Kisker, G. W. *The Disorganized Personality*. 2d. ed. New York: McGraw-Hill, 1972.

Klausmeier, H. J. and Ripple, R. E. *Learning and Human Abilities*. 3d. ed. New York: Harper & Row, 1971.

Klausner, S. Z., ed. *Why Man Takes Chances: Studies in Stress Seeking*. Garden City: Doubleday Anchor Books, 1968.

Knight, J. A. *Conscience and Guilt*. New York: Appleton-Century-Crofts, 1969.

Krech, D., Crutchfield R. S. and Ballachey, E. L. *Individual in Society*. New York: McGraw-Hill, 1962.

Kuhlen, R. G. and Thompson, G. G., eds. *Psychological Studies of Human Development*. 2d ed. New York: Appleton-Century-Crofts, 1963.

Larson, B., et. al. *Groups That Work*. Grand Rapids: Zondervan, 1967.

Lazarus, R. S., Averill, J. R. and Opton, E. M., Jr. "Towards a Cognitive Theory of Emotion." *Feelings and Emotions*. Edited by M. B. Arnold. New York: Academic Press, 1970, 207-32.

Lazarus, A. *Behavior Therapy and Beyond*. New York: McGraw-Hill, 1971.

Leib, J. W. "Teaching Machines and Programmed Instruction: Areas of Application." *Psychological Bulletin* 67 (1967): 12-26.

Leibowitz, H. W. *Visual Perception*. New York: Macmillan, 1965.

Lewin, K., Lippitt, R. and White, R. K. "Patterns of Aggressive Behavior in Experimentally Created 'Social Climates,'" *Journal of Social Psychology* 10 (1939); 271-299.

Lewis, C. S. *Miracles*. London: Fontana Books, 1947.

Lindgren, H. C. *An Introduction to Social Psychology*. New York: Wiley, 1969.

Lippitt, R. and White, R. K. "An Experimental Study of Leadership and Group Life." *Readings in Social Psychology*. 3d.ed. Edited by E. E. Maccoby, T. M. Newcomb, and E. L. Hartley. New York: Holt, 1958.

Maccoby, E. E., Newcomb, T. M. and Hartley, E. L., eds. *Readings in Social Psychology*. 3d. ed. New York: Holt, Rinehart and Winston, 1958.

Mager, R. F. *Preparing Instructional Objectives*. Palo Alto: Fearon, 1962.

Mains, D. *Full Circle*. Waco: Word, 1972.

Maslow, A. H. *Motivation and Personality*. 2d. ed. New York: Harper & Row, 1970.

Matarazzo, J. D. "The Interview." *Handbook of Clinical Psychology*. Edited by B. B. Wolman. New York: McGraw-Hill, 1965, 403-50.

McGuire, W. J. "Inducing Resistance to Persuasion." *Advances in Experimental Social Psychology*. vol. 1. Edited by L. Berkowitz. New York: Academic Press, 1964.

— — —. "A Vaccine for Brainwash." *Psychology Today* 3 (1970): 36-39, 63-64.

MacKay, D. M., ed. *Christianity in a Mechanistic Universe: and Other Essays.* Downers Grove: Inter-Varsity Press, 1965.

McLaughlin, R. W. *Communication for the Church.* Grand Rapids: Zondervan, 1968.

Mednick, S. A. *Learning.* Englewood Cliffs: Prentice-Hall, 1964.

Meehl, P., et. al. *What, Then, is Man?* St. Louis: Concordia, 1958.

Moberg, D. O. *The Church as a Social Institution.* Englewood Cliffs: Prentice-Hall, 1962.

— — —. "The Manipulation of Human Behavior: A Sociologist's Perspective." *Journal of the American Scientific Affiliation* 22 (Mar. 1970): 14-17.

Mowrer, O. H. *The Crisis in Psychiatry and Religion.* New York: Van Nostrand, 1961.

— — —. *Morality and Mental Health.* Chicago: Rand McNally, 1967.

Munn, N. L., Fernald, L. D., Jr. and Fernald, P. S. *Introduction to Psychology.* 2d. ed. Boston: Houghton-Mifflin, 1969.

Neuringer, C. and Michael, J. L. *Behavior Modification in Clinical Psychology.* New York: Appleton-Century-Crofts, 1970.

Norbeck, E., Price-Williams, D. and McCord, W. M., eds. *The Study of Personality: An Interdisciplinary Appraisal.* New York: Holt, Rinehart & Winston, 1968.

Oates, W. E. and Lester, A. D. *Pastoral Care in Crucial Human Situations.* Valley Forge: Judson, 1969.

Omstead, M. S. *The Small Group.* New York; Random House, 1959.

Outler, A. *Psychiatry and the Christian Message.* New York: Harper and Brothers, 1954.

Packard, V. *The Status Seekers.* New York: Giant Cardinal, 1961.

Papageorges, D. "Warning and Persuasion." *Psychological Bulletin* 70 (1968): 271-82.

Penfield, W. *The Excitable Cortex in Conscious Man.* Springfield: Charles C. Thomas, 1958.

Perske, R. "The Pastoral Care and Counseling of Families of the Mentally Retarded." *Pastoral Psychology* 19 (Nov. 1968): 21-28.

Petersen, S. D. "The Pastoral Care of Parents of Mentally Retarded Persons." *Pastoral Psychology* 13 (Sept. 1962): 37-44.

Pressey, S. L. "A Simple Apparatus which Gives Tests and Scores—and Teaches." *School and Society* 23 (1926): 373-76.

Razran, G. "Partial Reinforcement of Salivary CR's in Adult Human Subjects: Preliminary Study." *Psychological Reports* 1 (1955): 409-16.

Reid, C. *Groups Alive—Church Alive: The Effective Use of Small Groups in the Local Church.* New York: Harper & Row, 1969.

Richards, L. O. *Creative Bible Study.* Grand Rapids: Zondervan, 1970.

Roberts, D. E. *Psychotherapy and a Christian View of Man.* New York: Charles Scribner's Sons, 1950.

Rogers, C. "The Nature of Man." *The Nature of Man in Theological and Psychological Perspective.* Edited by Simon Doniger. New York: Harper, 1962.

Rokeach, M. "Persuasion that Persists." *Psychology Today* 5 (Sept. 1971): 68-71, 92.

Rosnow, R. L. "Poultry and Prejudice." *Psychology Today* 5 (Mar. 1972): 53-56.

and Robinson, E. J., eds. *Experiments in Persuasion.* New York: Academic Press, 1967.

Roth, R. H. "Student Reaction to Programmed Learning." *Phi Delta Kappan.* (Mar. 1963): 278-81.

Russell, B. *Why I am not a Christian: And Other Essays on Religion and Related Subjects.* New York: Simon and Schuster, 1957.

Secord, P. F. and Backman, C. W. *Social Psychology.* New York: McGraw-Hill, 1964.

Simpson, G. E. and Yinger, J. M. *Racial and Cultural Minorities.* New York: Harper & Row, 1958.

Singer, J. L. *Daydreaming: An Introduction to the Study of Inner Experience.* New York: Random House, 1966.

Skinner, B. F. "The Science of Learning and the Art of Teaching." *Harvard Educational Review* 24 (1954): 86-97.

— — —. "Teaching Machines." *Science* 128 (1958): 969-77.

— — —. *The Technology of Teaching.* New York: Appleton-Century-Crofts, 1968.

— — —. *Walden Two.* New York: Macmillan, 1948.

Smith, W. I. and Moore, J. W., eds. *Programmed Learning.* Princeton: Van Nostrand, 1962.

Stark, R., Foster, B. D., Glock, C. Y. and Quinley, H. "Sounds of Silence." *Psychology Doday* 3 (Apr. 1970): 38-41, 60-61.

Strong, A. H. *Systematic Theology.* Old Tappan: Revell, 1907.

Strong, E. K., Jr. "Change of Interests with Age." *Psychological Studies of Human Development.* 2d. ed. Edited by R. G. Kuhlen and G. G. Thompson. New York: Appleton-Century-Crofts, 1963, 234-42.

— — —. "Permanence of Interest Scores Over 22 Years." *Journal of Applied Psychology* 35 (1951): 89-91.

— — —. "Satisfactions and Interests." *American Psychologist* 13 (1958): 449-56.

Strunk, O., Jr. *Readings in the Psychology of Religion.* New York: Abingdon, 1959.

Stubblefield, H. W. "On being a Pastor to the Mentally Retarded." *The Journal of Pastoral Care* 24 (June, 1970): 98-108.

Telford, E. W. and Sawrey, J. M. *The Exceptional Individual: Psychological and Educational Aspects.* Englewood Cliffs: Prentice-Hall, 1967.

Tenney, M. C. *New Testament Survey.* Grand Rapids: Eerdmans, 1961.

Terman, L. M. "The Discovery and Encouragement of Exceptional Talent." *American Psychologist* 9 (June, 1954): 221-30.

— — —. and Merrill, M. A. *Stanford-Binet Intelligence Scale.* Boston: Houghton-Mifflin, 1960.

— — —. and Oden, M. H. "The Gifted Group at Mid-Life." *Genetic Studies of Genius.* vol. 5. Stanford: Stanford University Press, 1959.

Thielicke, H. *The Trouble with the Church: A Call for Renewal.* New York: Harper & Row, 1965.

Thompson, R. F. *Foundations of Physiological Psychology.* New York: Harper & Row, 1967.

Thouless, R. H. *An Introduction to the Psychology of Religion.* 3d. ed. New York: University Press, 1971.

Tournier, P. *Guilt and Grace*. New York: Harper & Row, 1962.

Towns, E. L. and Groff, R. *Successful Ministry to the Retarded*. Grand Rapids: Baker, 1971.

Trabasso, T. "Pay Attention." *Psychology Today* 2 (Oct. 1968): 30-36.

Travers, R. M. E. *Essentials of Learning*. 3d. ed. Riverside: Macmillan, 1972.

Trueblood, E. *The Humor of Christ*. New York: Harper & Row, 1964.

— — —. *The Incendiary Fellowship*. New York: Harper & Row, 1967.

Tyler, L. E. *The Psychology of Human Differences*. rev. ed. New York: Appleton-Century-Crofts, 1965.

Ulrich, R., Stachnik T. and Mabry, J., eds. *Control of Human Behavior*. Glenview: Scott, Foresman, 1966.

Vernon, M. D. *Human Motivation*. Cambridge: University Press, 1969.

— — —. *The Psychology of Perception*. Baltimore: Penguin, 1962.

Watson, J. B. and Rayner, R. "Conditioned Emotional Reactions." *Journal of Experimental Psychology* 3 (1920): 1-14.

Wheatherhead, L. D. *Psychology, Religion and Healing*. London: Hodder Stoughton, 1951.

Webb, W. B. *Sleep: An Experimental Approach*. New York: Macmillan, 1968.

White, R. K. and Lippitt, R. "Leader Behavior and Member Reaction in Three Social Climates." *Group Dynamics*. Edited by D. Cartwright and A. Zander. Evanston: Row, Peterson, 1953.

Wilkinson, T. A. and Collins, G. R. "Programmed Religious Instruction: Theory, Research, and Application." Unpublished manuscript. Trinity Evangelical Divinity School, Deerfield, Ill. 1971.

Wolff, R. *The Meaning of Loneliness*. Wheaton: Key, 1970.

Wolman, B. B., ed. *Handbook of Clinical Psychology*. New York: McGraw-Hill, 1965.

Wright, G. D. "A Further Note on Ranking the Important Psychologist." *American Psychologist* 25 (1970): 650-51.

Zuck, R. B. and Getz, G. A. *Christian Youth: An In-depth Study*. Chicago: Moody, 1968.

INDEX

A

accidents 33, 60
achievement 82-84
advertising, advertisers 40, 41-43, 108
American Psychological Association 14
anger 52, 54, 107
anxiety 35, 54, 59
aptitude 81-82
Asch, Solomon 101
attention 42-45
attitudes 13-14, 37, 107-109, 111
authority 127, 129

B

behavior 62, 130-131
Berkouwer, G. C. 131
Bible 122-123, 142
Blatz, William 51

C

Christ 74, 86, 99, 106, 107, 109, 112, 122, 123
Christian Education 14, 23, 31, 36, 65, 77, 80, 96
Christianity 121-143
chromosomes 74
Church 34-36, 61-65, 76, 79-80, 90, 94-96, 99-100
    underground 19
civil disobedence 86
coffee houses 86
communication 106, 113-115
conditioning (see learning)
conscience 131-133
contests 17
conversion 135-136
counseling 54, 77, 88, 128
cretin 74
crying 52

M

N

O

P